Godless Shakespeare

Shakespeare

NOW!

Series edited by: Simon Palfrey and Ewan Fernie

Godless Shakespeare

Eric S. Mallin

continuum

Continuum

The Tower Building
11 York Road
London
SE1 7NX
www.continuumbooks.com

80 Maiden Lane
Suite 704
New York
NY 10038

British Library Cataloguing-in-Publication Data
A catalogue record for this book is available from the British Library.

ISBN-10:   HB: 0-8264-9041-7
          PB: 0-8264-9042-5
ISBN-13:   HB: 9780826490414
          PB: 9780826490421

Library of Congress Cataloging-in-Publication Data
A catalog record for this book is available from the Library of Congress.

Typeset by BookEns Ltd, Royston, Herts
Printed and bound by Athenaeum Press Ltd, Gateshead, Tyne and Wear.

Contents

Acknowledgments

Even a small book such as this incurs large debts, and I am happy to say what they are.

Simon Palfrey and Ewan Fernie have been patient, inspiring, perceptive readers and hearty advocates. The book would not have come into being without them.

James Garrison was the department chair at the University of Texas at Austin during the writing of *Godless*; he helped supply material support as well as never-depleted, collegial generosity. And a word of thanks goes to Richard Flores, who provided a timely and helpful grant.

Gregory Foran gave indispensable research help, which took the form of shocking efficiency and comprehensiveness.

Johnny McCallister knows more about art and kindness than most people can, and it's my good fortune to have learned something from him.

Douglas Bruster's comments on the manuscript helped it make a lot more sense than it would have without him. I gleefully imported most of his excellent suggestions.

John Timpane wrote me a letter about *The Winter's Tale* that I wish I could have published under my name. But instead I shall just say that he has been a splendid informant about Shakespeare and about the religious point of view, as well as a wonderful friend, in need and deed.

Paul Howe is a heroic model of learning, humor, humanism, and agnostic, critical intelligence. I am so lucky to know him.

Dolora Chapelle-Wojciehowski showed me some ways I could think about the soul, and they improved me. Teaching a course with her on early modern atheism was a privilege and pleasure exceeded only by her friendship.

Hilary M. Schor has too many virtues to fit into a sentence, so I shall simply record my loving thanks to her.

And greatest gratitude:

To my sister Elissa, spirit guide;
Sonia Rosalie, my mother, best reader;
Donna, for her courage and sweet joy; and
Rebecca, my reason for faith.

General Editors' Preface

Shakespeare Now! represents a new form for new approaches. Whereas academic writing is far too often ascendant and detached, attesting all too clearly to years of specialist training, *Shakespeare Now!* offers a series of intellectual adventure stories: animate with fresh and often exposed thinking, with ideas still heating in the mind.

This series of 'minigraphs' will thus help to bridge two yawning gaps in current public discourse. First, the gap between scholarly thinking and a public audience: the assumption of academics that they cannot speak to anyone but their peers unless they hopelessly dumb-down their work. Second, the gap between public audience and scholarly thinking: the assumption of regular playgoers, readers, or indeed actors that academics write about the plays at a level of abstraction or specialization that they cannot hope to understand.

But accessibility should not be mistaken for comfort or predictability. Impatience with scholarly obfuscation is usually accompanied by a basic impatience with anything but (supposed) common sense. What this effectively means is a distrust of really thinking, and a disdain for anything that might unsettle conventional assumptions, particularly through crossing or re-drafting formal, political, or theoretical boundaries. We encourage such adventure, and base our claim to a broad audience upon it.

Here, then, is where our series is innovative: no compromising of the sorts of things that can be thought; a commitment to publishing powerful cutting-edge scholarship; *but* a conviction that these things are essentially communicable, that we can find a language that is enterprising, individual and shareable.

To achieve this we need a form that can capture the genuine challenge and vigour of thinking. Shakespeare is intellectually exciting, and so too are the ideas and debates that thinking about his work can provoke. But published scholarship often fails to communicate much of this. It is difficult to sustain excitement over the 80–120,000 words customary for a monograph: difficult enough for the writer, and perhaps even more so for the reader. Scholarly articles have likewise become a highly formalized mode not only of publication, but also of intellectual production. The brief length of articles means that a concept can be outlined, but its implications or application can rarely be tested in detail. The decline of sustained, exploratory attention to the singularity of a play's language, occasion, or movement is one of the unfortunate results. Often 'the play' is somehow assumed, a known and given thing that is not really worth exploring. So we spend our time pursuing collateral contexts: criticism becomes a belated, historicizing footnote.

Important things have got lost. Above all, any vivid sense as to why we are bothered with these things in the first place. Why read? Why go to plays? Why are they important? How does any pleasure they give relate to any of the things we labour to say about them? In many ways, literary criticism has forgotten affective and political immediacy. It has assumed a shared experience of the plays and then averted the gaze from any such experience, or any testing of it. We want a more ductile and sensitive mode of production; one that has more chance of capturing what people are really thinking and reading about, rather than what the pre-empting imperatives of journal or respectable monograph tend to encourage.

Furthermore, there is a vast world of intellectual possiblity – from the past and present – that mainstream Shakespeare criticism has all but ignored. In recent years there has been a move away from 'theory' in literary studies: an aversion to its obscure jargon and complacent self-regard; a sense that its tricks were too easily rehearsed and that the whole game has become one of diminishing returns. This has further encouraged a retreat into the supposed safety of historicism. Of course the best such work is stimulating, revelatory, and indispensable. But too often there is little trace of any struggle; little sense that the writer is coming at the subject afresh, searching for the most appropriate language or method. Alternatively, the prose is so labored that all trace of an urgent story is quite lost.

We want to open up the sorts of thinking – and thinkers – that might help us get at what Shakespeare is doing or why Shakespeare matters. This might include psychology, cognitive science, theology, linguistics, phenomenology, metaphysics, ecology, history, political theory; it can mean other art forms such as music, sculpture, painting, dance; it can mean the critical writing itself becomes a creative act.

In sum, we want the minigraphs to recover what the Renaissance 'essay' form was originally meant to embody. It meant an 'assay' – a trial or a test of something; putting something to the proof; and doing so in a form that is not closed-off and that cannot be reduced to a system. We want to communicate intellectual activity at its most alive: when it is still exciting to the one doing it; when it is questing and open, just as Shakespeare is. Literary criticism – that is, really thinking about words in action, plays as action – can start making a much more creative and vigorous contribution to contemporary intellectual *life*.

Simon Palfrey and Ewan Fernie

Introduction

Imagine an unearthly afterlife for characters in Shakespeare's plays.

In the most familiar Western version of the spiritual future, souls will fall or rise into a structure, a three-part ethical space: Hell, Purgatory, Heaven. Let me borrow that design for these imaginings.

Now, suppose Shakespeare's characters dwell in a universe not presided over by a knowable deity. How might we reckon their fates?

Here, in the ordered afterlife of a godless cosmos, are the psychic and spiritual characteristics of place and persons.

Hell

Occlusion; deception and deceptiveness for no end; infidelity to others, to self, and to love; bad faith in all things, or the most important ones; ambition without a justifiable or rational ideal or goal; deployment of language merely to deceive, or to produce only misdirection; utter opacity of motives, and reluctance or inability to examine them. The quality of cowardice at crucial moments, or of factitious generosity, piety, and heroism in the interest of self-glorification and at the severe, inevitable expense of others. Willingness to be used or obtuseness about becoming a tool of other interests. Theatricality/hypocrisy as a dead-end strategy. Helpless or reflexively devout response to the idea of divinity. Refusal to consider a godless universe.

Purgatory

Partial, spotted clarity; inability but potential to reach or express truth; wavering fidelity to self, love, or an ideal; commitment to self and other that does not primarily improve the world, but mainly one's position in it; an ignorant faith in positive outcomes, or an undeserved pessimism about negative ones; pained refusal or inability to make distinctions between moral, ethical, or even taxonomic categories. Cowardice and bravery in oscillation, making a mess of purposes and a random hash – some ways good, some not – of outcomes. Theatricality as ambiguous blessing to self and others. Skeptical but adaptive response to the chance of godlessness.

Heaven

Lovely if not perfect clarity about motive, or, at least, reluctance to impugn others for their motives and similar reluctance to self-aggrandize or self-congratulate without cause; attempt, usually mediated by joy or revelation, to speak truth as consciously known, or, in extreme circumstances, to hide or alter a truth that is destructive; ability to attract devoted and uncoerced followers, or to exist in splendid isolation without the need for acolytes. Theatricality as inspiration, access to transcendence, and deep, paradoxical significance. Triumphant, productive taking-in of unbelief.

* * * * * * * *

A dinner party for Stephen Greenblatt. The Shakespeare critic and biographer is in town for a lecture. Months later, one of the hosts recalls the occasion and a discussion on the way to the fête. The chat engages the possibility of an atheist Shakespeare. With some polite hesitation, Professor Greenblatt asks: 'But doesn't every gesture of unbelief articulate itself within the frame of a sectarian structure that determined it?' (He really did say this, or something like it.)[1]

In other words, isn't the idea of Renaissance unbelief artificial at best, in that it only arises within the conceptual borders of religion itself – as a heresy, a perversion, or some other already summoned, negated, and reviled possibility?

The question subtly revises an older one, put most famously by Lucien Febvre: is atheism in the Renaissance even possible?[2] True, an active and vocal godlessness would have been so ill advised as to be suicidal, and may not be much in evidence at the time. But once we argue the unthinkability or impotence of Believing Otherwise, we exclude compelling possibilities: that religion constructs itself against the backdrop of atheism, not the other way around; that organized belief always tries to fend off and neutralize the threat of other systems, including the absence of systems; and that Shakespeare might (because of his remarkable deftness and love of complication) operate in a way that escapes the inevitability of such doctrinal containment as Greenblatt implies.

My goal in this book is to suggest some of the ways in which Shakespeare's beliefs, when they can be inferred, show a mind and a spirit uncontained by orthodoxy. His faith or spiritual inclinations cannot be predicted or bound by the religious habits of thought endemic to much of his culture. While the symbolic, thematic elements of Christianity certainly find their way into his work, Shakespeare activates these features in decidedly irreligious or ironic ways.

I considered organizing this book around particular tenets of religion that his theater undermines, or at least rethinks: God's omnipotence, the function of sacrifice, the meaning of conversion, the nature of miracles, life everlasting. However, the current structure, following as it does Dante's precedent of spiritual ascent, better fits my conviction about the potential enlightenment in atheist or heretical thought, particularly as that thought applies to Shakespeare. A kind of paradise awaits the renegade, the doubter, the founder of one's own sect of self. This heaven lacks the cozy upholstery of clouds and choiring angels, and indeed has no actual

geography. The paradise I posit is a brightly lit theoretical or philosophical landscape, a step up from the shadow zone of purgatory
(where newly or potentially unbelieving characters take residence),
and several parsecs above the blind hell to which Shakespeare's
unthinking believer belongs.

*   *   *   *   *   *   *   *

The *Divine Comedy* structure in some sense affirms the very thing
my title refutes: the idea of a universe under the aegis of a controlling, rationalizing intelligence. For the purposes of this book,
Shakespeare is that mind, and like Dante's pilgrim on the path to
discovery, my job consists largely of divining the disposition of
selected characters in their purely imaginary afterlife.

For Dante, the regions of Inferno, Purgatory, and Paradise articulate the mind and intentionality of God, sinners and saved disposed
as he wishes, according to the complementary dictates of free will
and historical luck. ('Luck' as in 'fortune dependent on when and
where you lived and died': if before Christ, before you could be bap-
tized, or away from the region of His influence, you are generally out
of luck.) But in a secular, theatrical world, judgment resides not with
God, or even entirely with the author, but with other characters, the
audience, the reader. Dante's triple-tiered format conveniently provides a schema of my responses to some figures on stage, and the
relative position of these figures in what I see as Shakespeare's
implicit spiritual and ethical hierarchy. But as my descriptions of
each region suggest, this book depends on inversion: Hell represents
expressions of (ineffectual, deluded) religious faith in Shakespeare;
Purgatory sets out more skeptical and mixed positions; and Heaven,
the most intense articulations of godlessness.

Because the theater is built to the scale of our judgments, not
God's, our discriminations must rise to the challenge of
Shakespeare's complexity, must embrace the generosity and cool
cynicism of his fine moral gradations.[3] For this task, traditional religious understandings are inappropriate. In comparison to

Shakespeare's expansive and unpredictable ethics, divine judgment itself – the assessment of salvation and damnation – appears clumsy, crude. The playwright has a way of bestowing heroic qualities on the impotent or reprobate, and limning infamy and depravity in the gifted and fortunate; he can thereby gratify a sense of justice that is not boxed in by the absolutism of God's (supposed) intentions. The complex ethics of the theater offer reason enough to entertain the notion of a godless Shakespeare.

In my reading, a Shakespearean hell would be populated by, among others, the self-consciously and self-puffingly virtuous, those whose belief in their own higher morality makes them incapable of insight, generosity, or truth-telling. Conversely, were a Shakespeare heaven to exist à la Dante, it would teem with figures whose actions may in the ordinary Christian scheme of things damn them, but whose knowledge of self or perception of cosmos comprises honesty, courage, and clarity enough to recommend them. In Shakespeare, wickedness can redeem and virtue become the repository of pathological self-interest; if we adjust our vision, a surprising, transformative, complex moral order comes into view.

Complexity can, however, yield unclarity, and, at times, Shakespeare's characters (and their imagined destinies) do not merely transvalue given orthodoxies; sometimes they remain morally or ethically obscure. Because of the difficulty or at least the frequent uncertainty of judgment in the plays, I follow Catholic cosmology to include the symbolic transitional space of Purgatory. Its Shakespearean inhabitants would not be scarce. There we might find the generally objectionable Portia from *The Merchant of Venice*, who impressively recognizes her own ethical lapses: 'If to do were as easy as to know what were good to do, chapels had been churches, and poor men's cottages princes' palaces' (1.2.12–14). Yet she culpably indulges her worst impulses, and feels proud of them: 'This comes too near the praising of myself' (3.4.22), and later, after ruining Shylock: 'So shines a good deed in a naughty world' (5.1.91). Disgusting, smug, but she *has* averted a murder. The generally damnable Othello somehow achieves the apex of Renaissance Christian cultural faith – Turk-killing – as he commits the greatest act of Christian sin – self-slaughter. Falstaff, a terrible pleasure, hilariously mocks Hal's pompous heroism, tainted inheritance, and unearned piety, and (as part of the mockery) sends 150 men to their deaths with only a confession that he has used the King's powers of military impressment 'damnably'. For each of these characters, ethical clarity, occlusion, and religiosity coexist and twine.

This intricacy, which can sponsor a sense of moral uncertainty or even detachment, has long led some to conclude that Shakespeare suffered no great overflow of sectarian feeling or traditional piety. Eighteenth-century critic Joseph Ritson, for instance, maintained that Shakespeare was free of the 'reigning superstition of the time,' and 'addicted to no system of bigotry' – by which he means 'religion.'[4] Shakespeare often engages biblical language and Christian doctrine to elaborate a dramatic point, but the claim that he was not addicted to religious bigotry speaks to a common acknowledgment that the plays do not devote themselves to devoutness, do not seek to instill in the audience a Christian reverence.

Somewhat more recently, George Santayana went further, admitting the possibility of a Shakespearean atheism:

> But for Shakespeare, in the matter of religion, the choice lay between Christianity and nothing. He chose nothing; he chose to leave his heroes and himself in the presence of life and of death with no other philosophy than that which the profane world can suggest and understand . . .
>
> Shakespeare's world . . . is only the world of human society. The cosmos eludes him; he does not seem to feel the need of framing that idea. He depicts human life in all its richness and variety, but leaves that life without a setting, and consequently without a meaning.[5]

To Santayana, Shakespeare's atheism records mainly selective attention; the philosopher views this as a flaw, arguing that for the dramatist, the compelling elements of life are not cosmic action and the prime mover, but local or historical actions and those who are thereby moved.

The contention that richly depicted human life, in lacking a 'setting,' consequently must lack a meaning, sounds odd to me; but Santayana may as well have been describing the work of any number of famous figures in the early modern period: Machiavelli and Rabelais, Montaigne and Ralegh, Vanini and Marlowe. Agnostic and atheist possibilities in the early modern period mingled with curiously orthodox allegiances (see the work of Carlo Ginzburg, for instance[6]); and the attribution of 'atheism' to a writer was itself a mixed genre, bringing with it a complex of potent suspicions, base slanders, tart sarcasms, and actual perceived godlessness. Such conditions have begun to be explored by historians and literary scholars (David Wootton and Michael Hunter, Richard Popkin, Alan C. Kors, Jennifer M. Hecht, David Riggs, Robert N. Watson),[7] and their work gratifyingly corrects the considerable gaps in earlier views of 'the problem of unbelief.'

Unbelief was clearly possible in the Renaissance, and, as staged by Shakespeare, it furnishes a rich contrast and a goad to religious certainty. We can, for example, spot outbursts of atheist influence at one typically pivotal dramatic and theological moment: the encounter with death and the idea of the afterlife. We might expect in such a moment an unpolluted religious sentiment and autopilot piety. Yet that does not always occur. For example, in her wedding-night reverie about death and sex, Juliet imaginatively vaults her new husband into a firmament full of light and bare of holy neighbors (angels, saints, or grace's ministers):

> Come, gentle night, come, loving, black-brow'd night,
> Give me my Romeo, and, when I shall die,
> Take him and cut him out in little stars,
> And he will make the face of heaven so fine
> That all the world will be in love with night . . .
>
> (3.2.20–4)

For a girl with a good religious education (evidenced, ironically, by the sexy 'holy palmer' sonnet that she creates with Romeo at their first meeting), Juliet speaks lines that have nothing of Christianity about them. Her words remind us, as does her later suicide, that she takes surprisingly little account of divinity. Indeed, the language of the elementary school art project ('cut him out in little stars') seems, if anything, innocently pagan. Juliet charitably wishes to share her postmortem love with the world; but her hope that all the world will be in love with night sounds like she's forgetting something.

It's the same thing that slips Claudio's mind as he faces execution in *Measure for Measure*. Speaking from his jail cell to his sister, the novitiate Isabel, Claudio begs her to use what power she has to save him. No, not the power of prayer for aid in salvation. Rather, he asks her to sleep with the substitute duke (Angelo) in exchange for a pardon. She reasonably refuses, yet can (or wishes to) offer in response no comforting bromides about heaven or eternal justice. He then reminds her, in one of the most extraordinary (and Dantean) speeches in Shakespeare, of what he may be facing:

CLAUDIO.   Death is a fearful thing.
ISABEL.   And shamed life a hateful.
CLAUDIO.   Ay, but to die, and go we know not where;
              To lie in cold obstruction, and to rot;
              This sensible warm motion to become
              A kneaded clod; and the delighted spirit
              To bathe in fiery floods, or to reside
              In thrilling region of thick ribbed ice;
              To be imprison'd in the viewless winds
              And blown with restless violence round about
              The pendant world; . . .

                        . . .
              . . . 'tis too horrible!

                                    (3.1.115–27, passim)

Like Juliet, Claudio has no discernible relationship with God.

Isabel's response – 'Alas, alas!' – briefly abandons that relationship, too. When Claudio considers the afterlife, agonized thoughts cluster and crowd out redemptive hopes: he cannot free his mind from the noxious myths of eternity that foreclose all comfort in the thought of dying. And after her 'alas,' Isabel recovers poorly, offering to 'pray a thousand prayers for thy death, | No word to save thee' (3.1.145–6). This exchange is not, on Shakespeare's part, skepticism or equivocal detachment. It is a picture of religion as terrified sadism, the product of faith's deep, frustrated inadequacy to meliorate the darkness, or to cope with the complexities of selves who are touched by desire, the law, loneliness, despair.

Claudio's fright about his fate briefly punctures Isabel's faith, or at least her ability to enjoin her brother to Christian sentiment. What happened to her beliefs?

In Isabel's case, and throughout the canon, we see spiritual convictions crumble under pressure. As godless Shakespeare frequently reminds us, such convictions – for brother and sister, or Juliet and the audience – are neither stable nor universal: one person's salvation is another's 'shamed life,' one's happy apotheosis is an audience's wasteful tragedy. And Shakespeare has no qualms about neutering the ethical potency or privilege of the spiritual, no interest in defending the moral highground or the emotional exemptions that so many godly people claim. He finds far more gripping the dramatic confrontation between faith and transgression.

In following the shape of Dante's *Divine Comedy* – a work that Shakespeare probably never read – I mean to recall a literary structure that arises from just such confrontation. 'Godless' Shakespeare, then, is a description of theatrical practice, not a biographical claim. Only off the margins of the text can we speculate about how practice and personal belief might interact.

For all of my suspicions here about Shakespeare's lack of assurance in the God and entrenched myths of Judeo-Christian culture, I have few doubts about two things. First, in his professional guise as a *popular* writer, Shakespeare sought to supply entertainment rather than offense – so there is little payoff for him in alienating his audience by dully clinging to or *overtly* disparaging one doctrine or another, or doctrine in and of itself. (Occasional bursts of insult against Puritans and Catholics do occur, of course, but such examples are usually mitigated by the characteristic Shakespearean density and sympathy.) And in a time when language against the established Church could incur imprisonment and execution, Shakespeare could not exactly assume the profile of a freethinking culture critic. So if his godless leanings were insufficiently articulated, that might have something to do with professional conditions as much as theological convictions.

Which leads me to my other certainty: Shakespeare discloses, fairly regularly, his belief in an occult world, one cheerfully or menacingly beyond rationality. Specifically, he buys into the notion of the soul, however theoretically troublesome that conviction becomes in a godless universe. The idea of a personal essence, the transcendent part of the self, animates his poetry and stagecraft. I would categorize such a belief as 'spirituality'. Let me also stipulate that spirituality and godlessness need not be antithetical. Santayana himself noted of the sex-and-art-obsessed Sonnets that they, 'as a whole, are spiritual; their passion is transmuted into discipline' ('Absence,' 151). Far from being an eternal or fixed experience, rigid and impersonal or corporate like religion, spirituality imagines the self reaching beyond the world it knows by means of what it knows, making a leap to otherness always factored by one's age, politics, capacity for love and hope, knowledge and fear – by the personal and cultural past, the guessed-at future. *Every earthly contingency shapes the spiritual.* Including, of course, atheist leanings and the fiction of divinity. I believe it is possible, as Jonathan Dollimore asserts, that 'spirituality survives in and as unbelief (only the sacrilegious truly understand the sacred),'[8] a proposition that *Godless Shakespeare* explores as we move to paradisal atheism.

At the core of Shakespearean godlessness lies the need to question received significances, to self-make meanings. Some, who make their own meanings, earn perdition. Still others form, from the center of their beliefs, a truer divinity than any on the books.

Part One

Hell

1 God's Bitch

Pericles

> How we laugh up here in heaven
> At the prayers you offer me.
> That's why I love mankind.

> Randy Newman, 'God's Song'

Years before she killed herself, a friend of mine said: 'I just don't think there's a benevolent core to the universe, Eric.'

Most theology contests that opinion, with varying degrees of success. Plaintive cries come from those who, amid tribulations, seek the benevolent core and find only loss and heartache. Why any god would sanction prolonged torment of faithful followers is a familiar question with no abidingly satisfactory answers from the Judeo-Christian tradition.

The Book of Job prompts the question. Job is a grateful patriarch, a believer in the God who has provided his good life. But that life soon changes radically and his trials begin when God boasts to Satan: Do you see my faithful servant? Satan scoffs, and braves God: since Job has been misfortune-proof, his devotion must be simple and fragile. Put him to the test, he'll crumble. So unbeknownst to Job, God agrees to allow Satan to torture his faithful servant on a whim, on a bet. That alone should tell us something, not about God, about whom there is (Job eventually discovers) nothing to be known, but about how biblical scribes flirted with the abyss, confessing the incomprehensibility of fate, the inevitability and unjustifiability of suffering, and – rebelliously, explosively – the uselessness of the God-concept for an apperception of experience. The believer grows grievously afflicted: Job's family is killed, his body disintegrates, and then (worst of all – the people are always worst of all) he is tormented by 'friends' who relentlessly question his faith and virtue. The fact that Job's fortunes are eventually restored does not necessarily mitigate the harshness of the tale.

Jack Miles suggests that Job may well exceed its purposes – much, I think, the way the first nuclear reaction potentially exceeded the boundaries of containment, threatening a perpetual, universal conflagration, as Robert Oppenheimer feared.[1] Miles claims that Job was written 'only to bring smug and schematic Near Eastern wisdom to its knees before the unpredictable Lord of the Jews,' but yet may achieve 'a far broader subversion.'[2]

That subversion is the demolition of the idea of sane grounds for belief: specifically, the idea of a caring God who protects his creations. An infinite, never-emptied well of suffering drowns faith; God's failure to care for the world or (especially) his most devout followers floods the space of belief.

For Job discovers (and, as Miles implies, the eponymous book discovers too) the demonic element in the divine prerogative. Forget the benevolent core: it may be actively hostile. Enfolded but not curtailed – indeed, set free – the wicked principle at the heart of divinity radically shifts the moral of the story. If we think of the tale as meaning something like 'keep your faith through adversity, you will be rewarded,' another, more potent view of the piece might paraphrase it: 'you, lowly, cannot hope to fathom or influence God; you are without power, status, or meaning in a randomly hostile universe.'

The entire baroque and brittle architecture of holiness might well cave in on itself as the implications of the Job exemplum reverberate. Since suffering has no rationale, it has no morality or ethics either. In Shakespeare's plays, obstacles to belief can seem insuperable, prolonged trials conjuring the possibility of a justifiable, indeed inevitable, atheism. Of the numerous Job echoes in the Shakespeare canon, none borrows more pointedly than *King Lear* the notion of relentlessly unintelligible and possibly hostile divine or cosmic forces. Gone is the providential optimism of triumphant Tudor forebears in the history plays; belief sours, a bad jest: 'As flies to wanton boys are we to th' gods: | They kill us for their sport' (4.1.36–7). And in other plays, mainly tragedies and problem comedies, radical reversals of fortune or station alienate a formerly grateful humanity from devoutness or obedience. *Timon of Athens* pictures a man whose fall from great to awful fortune produces a satirical, godless despair of the kind that Job avoids; in *Antony and Cleopatra*, the hero is said to lose the favor of the god Hercules, perhaps as a result of Antony's bad faith or worse luck. In the plays, belief recoils at misfortune, flagging the radical, Job-like possibility that the idea about God, or God's meanings, needs revising.

Job at least has no questions about the existence of a divine force, which speaks out of a whirlwind in the questioner's own tongue – even if that force does him active harm and fails to restore all that Satan had destroyed. For those who suffer what seems like causeless misery, who fear the absence of that benevolent core, the confirmation of a cosmic torturer would seem to provide a mixed comfort at best. Yet oddly enough, for some, it provides all the comfort they need. A perverse, angry, or hostile presence is better than a void.

* * * * * * * *

A good thing happens after many long and miserable trials. As with Job, that thing is really only the establishment or the restitution of a *norm*: a home, or family, or a position and a place. Yet the one good, which suddenly reassembles a fractured life, seems to amend all the wretchedness: 'So the LORD blessed the latter end of Job more than his beginning' (Job 42.12). Praise heaven.

This toxic illogic authorizes so much worship and underwrites so many theodicies that one might think that the capacity for reason disqualified a person from religious feeling. Who would be happy in a paradise devised by a deranged creator, ever subject to mad whim and choiceless punishment? Although the irony of the restoration of losses (caused or endorsed by the very divinity expecting such gratitude) is downright virulent, still God is good, and now all is as it should be. The years of pain and loss, of desolate questioning, are said to vanish, to matter no longer. But once you have passed from that phase of losses, and you take stock of what may be left to you, consider: this time, you have escaped. Later, you may not. And many never recover what they've lost. For most people, a force field prevents mercies from descending.

The title of this excursus expresses, however crudely, the combination of will-lessness and erotic subjection that encircles devotion's subscribers or bearers of faith. In this case, I refer to one of the great bitches in Shakespeare, which is to say, one of the most sympathetic victims of the posited higher powers and their manipulations: Pericles, King of Tyre.

The 'bitch' designation means to recall two issues. The first is that Job-like awareness of being God's plaything, one to which the creator is not emotionally attached – of being entirely and essentially *subjected*. The second is that erotic trafficking in which Pericles partakes, no matter how he tries to avoid it, and which further subjects him as it becomes an inextricable part of his fate.

The plot involves the hero's serial misfortunes, all of which he suffers passively and uncomprehendingly. Pericles falls in love and is threatened with death, falls into exile and shipwreck, meets someone new and marries her but (he thinks) sees her die in childbirth, suffers storms at sea and then, after long trials, joyously reunites with his daughter and miraculously, if a shade less joyously, with his not-dead wife. What makes the plot more than ordinarily interesting is the atmosphere of sexual victimage that informs it.

Pericles is obsessed with incest, and Pericles is, too. It follows him around like his shadow, shaping every aspect of his adventures and image. The inaugural episode in the life of the hero is a courtship test: he tries to win the hand of Antiochus's nameless daughter. To do so, he must solve a dangerous riddle – dangerous because the suitors who have failed to solve it (or perhaps, politely refused to) have been put to death. Antiochus threatens the new suitor with a charming vista of the skulls of failed princes: they 'with dead cheeks advise thee to desist | For going on death's net, whom none resist' (1.1.39–40). Pericles gives the absolutely correct reading in response: 'I thank thee, who hath taught | My frail mortality to know itself' (41–2).

Correct, but on some level not understood: although the conundrum may result in his death, Pericles skates on a frozen surface of meaning. The riddle he reads is framed in the voice of the daughter, and it seems at first entirely transparent; we wonder why no one has solved it, or, more pressingly, why the king would be willing even to let the riddle be spoken aloud:

> I sought a husband, in which labor
> I found that kindness in a father.
> He's father, son, and husband mild;
> I mother, wife – and yet his child:
> How they may be, and yet in two,
> As you will live, resolve it you.

> (1.1.66–71)

The play soon becomes all about preventing the tragic potential of incest – the complete, secret satisfaction that the father unlawfully takes in the daughter. Shakespeare exchanges (but cannot abandon) this wicked and oft-returning fantasy for the fiction of Pericles's richer emotional fulfillment with an adult wife and marriageable daughter. But oh, what torments the gods' bitch undergoes in order to secure this exchange. Because to evade the incest scenario which inaugurates the plot also means evading something elemental, primal: death, which cannot be evaded for long. In his final sermon, John Donne makes a relevant figural connection between the idea behind Antiochus's riddle and the reality of mortality:

Miserable riddle, when the same worm must be my mother, my sister and myself! Miserable incest, when I must be married to my mother and my sister, and be both father and mother to my own mother and sister, beget and bear that worm which is all that miserable penury; when my mouth shall be filled with dust, and the worm shall feed, and feed sweetly, upon me . . .[3]

Pericles has asked for help from 'You gods, that made me man, . . . | That have inflam'd desire in my breast | To taste the fruit of yon celestial tree | (Or die in th' adventure)' (1.1.19–22), and thus seems to perceive the connection or conflation of his humanity, his desire, his desire for transcendence, and his death. His 'inflam'd desire' for Edenic knowledge and the death he will suffer as a result of knowing *what he already knows* – the danger of transgression – are themselves the curses of the gods he supplicates. He hears the incest riddle, his 'frail mortality' somehow not recognizing itself, and desire for Antiochus's daughter redemptively flies at once: 'For he's no man on whom perfections wait | That, knowing sin within, will touch the gate' (1.1.79–80).

Let us distinguish three levels of meaning to Antiochus's riddle: denotative, connotative, annotative. Call the first the *reply*: Pericles reads 'I sought a husband, in which labor | I found that kindness in a father,' and the only plausible *reply* is: 'OK, I get it, you're sleeping with your pa.' The puzzle is too open and obvious, too denotative (especially given the putative shame of the action it describes) to rise to the standing of a genuine riddle, and a strangeness thus attends the pretense of interpretive difficulty. The second-level, connotative meaning might be called the *answer*. Antiochus's conundrum and the 'miserable riddle' that Donne delivers overlap in one plausible answer: death. Mortality itself (as Pericles was warned) is the connotative figure beneath and surrounding the incest image, for incest causes the loss of all boundaries and propriety, enclosing the family and begetting that worm (through barrenness, and no-difference) that, as the opening lines of the riddle tell us, will 'feed | On mother's flesh which did me breed' (1.1.64–5). Pericles's story begins with a miserable riddle whose *answer* is death – not, as he thinks, merely

incest, the signifier of death. And yet a third level of response is possible, embedded in the enigma. Pericles has a reply (incest), and he
can just barely perceive the answer (death) – but the *solution* escapes
him.

That solution is the annotative subtext of the riddle, which is to
say, the answer to a question it does not know and could not ask.
This deep-structure problem is indicated by the three-into-one
form that it takes: father, son, husband is one man; mother, wife,
child is one woman. What confronts Pericles is an allegory of something he could not possibly grasp because historically he precedes it:
the supposedly redemptive power of the three-person God.

Strikingly, each signifier of the riddle is conspicuously transparent or matchable to a signified, except for one. We can see how the
daughter feeds 'on mother's flesh' (all children do); and it is obvious
how she is 'mother, wife – and yet his child,' having taken the
mother's place. But when she seemingly identifies Antiochus as
'father, son, and husband mild,' the incest identification stumbles.
If the daughter refers to Antiochus here, she has no explanation
whatsoever for 'son.' (Except as a creepy anticipation of the salvational daughter, Marina, who as Pericles says 'beget'st him who did
thee beget' (5.1.195).) In what way is the father the same as the son?
the riddle compels us to ask, and in this context, the immediate,
worldly answer comes: he is not. Her sleeping with him can in no
way transform the father into her son. But in another way, the solution is evident: father and son are effectively identical in hypostatic
union, when the father is God, and the son is Christ. The curious
solution to the more-curious riddle is not sexual, but theological.

Because I am concerned to write about a godless Shakespeare, the
reader should not think that I am recommending this solution as
key to the play. Quite the opposite. Buried in the riddle is a perfect
image for the kind of thing religion always does, the thing that Job
comes to realize: it leaves seekers of the truth helpless to understand,
because it either buries much-needed answers in riddles, or pretends
that there are much-needed answers. But more importantly, the

missing solution to a riddle about incest and death turns out to be God. Pericles himself sees a problem in the transcendent sphere as soon as he has heard the puzzle: 'O you powers! | That gives heaven countless eyes to view men's acts, | Why cloud they not their sights perpetually, | If this be true which makes me pale to read it?' (1.1.72–5). But better questions might be: If powers are there, why do they allow such acts? Why do they not extinguish all light from this false creation? And a better question yet: Who cares? So a king is having sex with his own daughter. It's gross, but what difference does it make in the broad scheme of things? None at all, except insofar as it threatens Pericles's life to know it. And insofar as the fact points to an absence of the sacred.

The missing solution of the riddle takes figurative form in the stream of resurrections the play conducts. After being forced to flee from the homicidal Antiochus, and after many dangers and miserable voyages, Pericles reunites with the family he believed he had lost forever. This one-sentence summary does cut out some spiritual events: Pericles is led to discover his wife, Thaisa, in Ephesus, courtesy of a vision from the goddess Diana; Thaisa is helped to revive by a remarkable physician, Cerimon, who trumpets his own 'virtue and cunning,' saying 'immortality attends' those attributes, 'Making a man a god' (3.2.26–31). Clearly, several perspectives on the spiritual world are available here, including an ironic one. Perhaps most ironic is the name of the wife, for 'Thaisa' is twice contaminated by illicit sexuality: 'Thais' was a legendary courtesan of Alexander the Great; and 'Thaise' is the *daughter* of the Pericles figure in Shakespeare's source text. Along these lines, Pericles's daughter Marina, sold to a brothel, preaches at and converts the customers – one of whom, alarmingly, is her future husband – to a new chastity. A 'Gentleman' says, after hearing her preach (which, incidentally, we never do), 'I'll do anything now that is virtuous; but I am out of the road of rutting forever' (4.5.8–9). If that weren't funny enough, her Bawd complains of Marina that 'she's able to freeze the god Priapus, and undo a whole generation' (4.6.3–4). The notion of freezing that particular god – making him *harder* – scarcely bodes well for her chaste effects on men. We cannot take Marina's 'divinity' too seriously because her reformative powers work against her. They beget that which her begot.

Francis Bacon inadvertently attacks belief when he acknowledges that one of the key causes of atheism is 'learned times, specially with peace and prosperity; for troubles and adversities do more bow men's minds to religion.'[4] Quite right: Pericles acquires faith in his desperation and, Job-like, is apparently rewarded for that faith and that desperation. But he ends by planning to celebrate his daughter's nuptials – she has no choice in these – and failing to notice that a twisted cosmic justice has temporarily and unintelligibly allowed him some happiness.

*   *   *   *   *   *   *   *

Where are the gods in all this? The two forms that divinity takes here, Neptune and Diana, signify respectively the immense potentialities of suffering (at sea) and the rewards of resistance (chastity). These figures, more characteristics than avatars, do not guarantee happy endings, in spite of virtue, sufferance, conversion, and reconciliation. Who can make such a guarantee? Only one figure in the story.

His name is Gower, and he is Shakespeare's choral voice, the famed medieval poet who wrote *Pericles*'s source text *Confessio Amantis*. Gower introduces the action, and provides the moral. He also entreats the audience to let the imagination work, fill up the stage and complete the gaps of space and time with mind: 'In your supposing once more put your sight' (5. ch. 21). His first appearance tells us something consequential about his function as a religious icon, one that merges magnificently with the literary figure; he announces:

> From ashes ancient Gower is come,
> Assuming man's infirmities,
> To glad your ear and please your eyes.

(1. Chorus 2–4)

Such Christological self-announcement, all for the sake of audience pleasure, explains what happens to religious faith in the play: it pours into theatrical experience. Resurrection occurs on our behalf to gratify sensory organs; our faith and imaginative devotion to completing a story cause what redemption the theatrical event affords, including the saving of otherwise musty tales and poets. The notion of Shakespeare's theater as a substitute church of images, compensatory perhaps for a moribund or suppressed Catholicism in England, has come lately to be something of an orthodox position, but that's not what I am arguing here.

For the theater to provide spiritual fulfillment, it must provide a workable, worldly model of mutuality, a form of semi-Pelagianism.[5] That medieval doctrine tries to amend Augustine's view of God's sovereign, overwhelming grace by modifying it with an idea of a participatory human will, necessarily functional and co-equal in our salvation. The semi-Pelagian theology offers a splendid secular model for the theater: the audience's interest and sympathies help create the world on stage and its fictions of redemption. Gower assumes man's infirmities – he takes human form, presupposes that men sin, and absorbs the infirmities he adopts – and in exchange, he will ask us to attend to and fill in the pleasing fictions of just the sort religion itself can deliver.

The word 'deliver' usefully signifies the overlap between the imaginative and the salvational. A word for birth and narrative, it also refers to redemption or gift. Marina conjoins the meanings when she reveals her own past to her father, a story told her by her nurse: 'My mother was the daughter of a king, | Who died the minute I was born, | As my good nurse Lychorida hath oft | Delivered weeping' (5.1.157–60). The nurse weeps the woe of a birth story, virtually gives birth to the tale, and it is a story that is itself salvational. Continuing the redemptive narrative theme, Pericles tells Marina, 'I will believe you by the syllable | Of what you shall deliver' (5.1.167–8), and later asks the godlike Cerimon, 'Will you deliver | How this dead queen re-lives?' (5.3.63–4). That these

deliveries depend on narratives ties them to the central narrator and
Phoenix-figure Gower, who controls and shapes the story, with the
help of the audience:

> At Ephesus the temple see,
> Our King and all his company.
> That he can hither come so soon
> Is by your fancies' thankful doom.
>
> (5.2.17–20)

Shakespeare takes the substitution of theatrical for eschatological
faith seriously; it is not that one stands for the other, but rather that
one *replaces* the other. That is, the presence of the redeemer is
almost invisible, buried in riddle. As a consequence of this functional godlessness, the literary narrator, our choral psychopomp,
becomes the only true redeemer of the play, capable authorially of
constructing redemption. He assumes our infirmities, helps to
'deliver' a tale of restitution, and, in the process, to deliver us.

As for Pericles, strapped into unthinking belief: hope and deliv-
erance come not from any god, who hides demonically in a riddle
of incest and death, who makes a bitch of faithful and desperate
men, but from theater and its priests. Hope arises in the blank space
theater asks us to fill, the sole core of benevolence in the
Shakespearean universe.

2 The Promise

Friar Laurence

Stunned by Juliet's evanescent beauty, the ghostly Father Friar
Laurence speaks these words when he first sees her:

> Here comes the lady. O, so light a foot
> Will ne'er wear out the everlasting flint;
> A lover may bestride the gossamers
> That idles in the wanton summer air,
> And yet not fall; so light is vanity.
>
> (*Romeo and Juliet*, 2.5.16–20)

A haunting disclosure. The Friar beholds her, and thinks at once of
her death. She will not survive the 'everlasting' stone, and only a
mineral eternity occurs to him. But his lament for her human life-
span comes bound up with lyrical resentment and scorn: she is
happy, buoyant with love.

No, with Vanity. Love has moral weight, but Vanity is airy, and
will not fall – yet it should. Hang clogs on the couple, and it will.
Quietly, he speaks again:

> *So light a foot as hers will never bear*
> *The weight of so much meaning. Now I know:*
> *She'll tread upon the sacred vows. I swear*
> *I'll turn them where their God would never go.*
> *The pretty boy came to me with his love,*
> *A jest, of course – or so I dreamed. Until*
> *She tripped here, and I planted prayers above.*

Gossamer vessels, both shall soon lie still
As loam. If Fortune's worth compares with kings',
Then she'll pour gold like lightning on my plan,
Disguised as improvised and desperate things;
I will do all that may become a man.
Holy I murmur: Give me so much power
To freight their lightness in this dusky hour.

3 Vienna Sausage: Or, Replacement Theology

Isabel

'Replacement theology' is an idea we owe to the Gospels and to early Christian anti-Semites such as Irenaeus and St. Augustine.[1] The point of the doctrine is that Christ and the Church effectively replace the Jews as the Lord's chosen. Augustine publicized a '"theory of substitution" whereby the New Israel of the church became a substitute of ancient Israel,' and 'explicitly stated that the title "Israel" belonged to the Christian church.'[2] Never mind that the view ignores what one writer calls 'the Jewishness of the Gospel.'[3] To the faithful, Jesus at once fulfills and erases the meanings of Old Testament prophecy and history by effectively acting as the telos of Jewish history, the ever-predicted Messiah. Inconveniently, most Jews disagreed. Trouble ensued.

In *Measure for Measure*, Vienna's ruler Vincentio vacates his dukedom and installs a substitute, 'the prenzie [precise, Puritanical] Angelo' (3.1.93), in his place. Vincentio (something of an historical King James substitute himself) plans to resurrect the best of the Old – that is, stricter adherence to the Law – as a way eventually of ushering in the New. In this play, the 'New' furnishes a surprise access of mercy *in contrast to* the draconian, legalistic, Puritanical measures that Angelo was installed to administer in the first place. Vincentio knows his Augustine, and he reasons that mercy needs to replace justice to show the shiny dispensation to best advantage. (Angelo, in his adherence to the Old Law, may remind the audience of an archetypal Jew, which Shakespeare and many of his contemporary playwrights seem to regard as an ancestor to the Puritan.) Angelo, whom the duke knows to be seriously flawed, is thus sacrificed – invested with a short-shelf-life power and meant only to act as foil for the ruler's virtues. Before long, exceeding even the dark expectations of him, Angelo imprisons and condemns to death a marginally innocent fornicator, and then attempts to extort sex from the prisoner's sister, Isabel, a Catholic novice. Angelo's rape attempt seems a tad crude as a way to tell us that the substitute lacks a certain political *je ne sais quoi*. But as a version of Augustinian ideology, it does yeoman's service. For the Duke's deputy stands in schematically for the notion that the New Law (Vincentio's impeccable mercy) should and must trump the Old (Angelo's perverted justice).

The Duke, however, problematizes this formula. Acting like the belated messiah he thinks he is, he takes a good long time to return to and amend the situation he vacated – although, unlike a messiah, he hovers about in disguise, an 'old fantastical Duke of dark corners' (4.4.156–7), as Lucio memorably puts it. But the Duke has a way of getting things to work out, even if they don't quite work out for everyone, and even if they involve actions well outside his rightful purview and prerogative, such as pretending to be a monk, taking confession, setting up deceptive romantic assignations, preparing condemned prisoners for death, and lying (several times, gratuitously) about their execution. Thus does Vincentio lacquer new meanings onto replacement theology, glossing its implications for political practice: holy men are substitutable, and God's representative can be traded out. Murderers can be pardoned and exchanged on a whim, the condemned replaced by just-executed criminals. For Vincentio, the Law has no absolute value, for he puts it to the service of random substitutions, coercive public relations, and religious dissimulation.

The replacement of the Duke with Angelo is but the first in the play's vertiginous cycle of disappointing switch-outs: Angelo for Escalus (the man who actually belongs in the substitute ruler role); Isabel's chastity for her brother Claudio's life; Mariana for Isabel, in secret; the murderer Barnardine for Claudio; then Ragozine the pirate for an unrepentant Barnardine. There are many more. The tireless substitutions suggest two things at once. First, because measure can be infinitely exchanged for measure, a law or role has no inherent, absolute truth. Substitutions can be conducted perpetually to benefit ideology, or power, or desire. The best instance of problematic replacement in the play is the mercy disbursed to Angelo, which substitutes the punishment he has earned. Vincentio has publicly challenged Isabel to forgive Angelo, despite her thinking that he has already had her brother Claudio killed. Her incoherent act of charity – 'because he didn't do *everything* he wanted to, you should pardon the man who lied, tried to bed me and killed my brother' – seems generous to a fault. But fault is the point, especially in an arena where politics and faith contaminate justice. Isabel, clearly, is caught not in a charity test (she passes that one) but in an interpretation or judgment quiz, which she messes up rather badly. She does show kindness to Mariana, who inexplicably wants Angelo for her husband. But because Angelo, overwhelmed by his exposure and humiliation, sincerely and repeatedly begs for death, to give him 'mercy' would not mean to spare his life so that he may marry and live miserably with the woman he wronged. Mercy, clearly, would be to kill him.

The second crucial suggestion inherent in the play's wild substitutions is the inescapable, subversive analogy. Because mercy and torment are fungible in Vienna, and justice a random element, politicians clearly cannot live up to absolute truths. But perhaps such truths simply do not exist. As God's earthly substitutes, dukes and deputies are also in some measure God's earthly *duplicates*, and maybe the duplication is more accurate than we thought. 'Mortality and mercy in Vienna' (1.1.44) are every bit as arbitrary, idiotic, and failed as mortality and mercy anywhere in the world, as a result of God's dictates and defects. The virtual absence, the empty chair, the monk's cowl with a false monk inside become fine figures for the ruling divine inadequacy.

The political leader as God's substitute, with his obvious flaws in morality and judgment, troubles ideas of God as much as ideas of the ruler. Furthermore, the failed surrogacies of this play analogically point to the deep inadequacy of surrogacy itself as a theology. Where the New botches mercy and justice just like the Old, we can spy a slant critique of the limited efficacy of Christianity, and of Christ in particular, to improve the world. For Christ is the substitute par excellence.

Indeed, the idea of the substitute establishes Christianity. Christ represents the symbolic sufferer for all humanity's transgressions, and his religion is the belated, replacement–fulfillment of Judaism. More particularly, the savior's bio-theological origins as a human divinity speak directly to the notion of the stand-in:

> The central fact of the incarnation may be seen as an instance of surrogacy. Mary, after all, was married to Joseph, yet she deliberately and explicitly consented to bear a child 'for God.' That is, she agreed to allow one of her eggs to be fertilized miraculously 'by the Holy Spirit,' to carry the child thus conceived to term, and to give that child up when the time came, so that he could devote himself to his real Father's business (Lk. 2.49).[4]

Juliet's pregnancy, which heralds Claudio's difficulties in Vienna, lacks this holy investiture. But even though she does not carry a heavenly child, she is at least a proximate cause of wholesale changes in the culture, and her childbearing inaugurates the central 'measure for measure' of the play: a life for a life. For her fetus causes the death – or (theoretically) threatens the life – of its father. This plot line is an analogue for hardcore replacement theology, where the birth of Christ (theoretically) causes the death of Judaism. Even if a Christian does not adopt the particular tenets of replacement theology, her belief feeds on surrogacy in the ordinary course of things. For in its best and worst guises, surrogacy is another name for *sacrifice*, the *sine qua non* of Christianity.

Vienna (whose laws, like sausage, we would not wish to see processed) has adopted surrogacy as a political strategy and technology, and thus it has also put into civic play the sacrificial model. Sacrifice is holy *replacement*, commensurability as a sacred act. But Shakespeare doubts its worth, or, at least, sees it as non-transferrable to the strictly human sphere (as we shall see with his several pointedly unsuccessful Christ figures). The problem with sacrifice, as with surrogacy in general, inheres in its poor arithmetic: is this thing *really* commensurate with that? Look at Isabel's knee-jerk endorsement of the Duke's bed trick, her willingness to sacrifice someone else's sexual and ethical integrity to avoid sacrificing her own. And compare that assent to her refusal to stand in for Claudio – her absolute denial of the commensurability of her physical virginity (which she interprets as her soul) for his life. She endorses in one context a transgression – covert fornication between Angelo and Mariana – that she reviles in another – namely Claudio's punishable sex with Juliet. The theology and politics of substitution have baffled her. The bed trick to which she contributes (setting up Angelo to think he's sleeping with her, while he's actually having sex with Mariana) shows her in unflattering light, reflecting as it does the same charge she had aimed at her brother: 'Thy sin's not accidental, but a trade. | Mercy to thee would prove itself a bawd, | 'Tis best that thou diest quickly' (3.1.148–50). Her notion of erotic sacrifice goes only so far: her sexuality is the vanishing point of her charity.

Her reward for this limitation is to suffer as a substitute, and a sacrifice, herself.

As Duke Vincentio's last-minute erotic choice, she becomes the play's own offering to the very idea of surrogacy. Shakespeare makes her a literary or genre stand-in for all the substitutions the Duke has performed throughout: she becomes the necessary prop for the happy marital ending. Angelo's desire for her finally has been ratified and substituted *as* the Duke's. As the target of this substitution, Isabel cannot manage the heavenly mother's neat trick of being both holy vessel and inculpable love slave. It isn't often that Shakespeare punishes a 'good' character so directly, but Isabel (who has shown not the slightest erotic interest in the Duke) genuinely can be faulted for repeatedly and conspicuously failing to live up to her own principles and failing also to reckon with her physical desires. In her response to Angelo's rapine extortion, she answers with an embodied, masochistic passion of her own:

> . . . were I under the terms of death,
> Th'impression of keen whips I'ld wear as rubies,
> And strip myself to death, as to a bed
> That longing have been sick for, ere I'ld yield
> My body up to shame.

> (2.4.100–4)

Or as a student wondered about these lines: 'if that's how she says no, what would yes sound like?'[5]

The play never tells us. For her lack of charity, her misunderstanding of the foundational ideal of Christian surrogacy, Isabel receives her punishment on earth: an enforced marriage to the Duke, who will, at the last, accept no substitutes. Silenced, Isabel – in the nun's case now, seen but unheard – loses her religion.

4 Crackers

Titus

SISTER ANNE.	Hello, children. I'm Sister Anne. And I'll be teaching you so that you can all receive your first communion!
STAN (*scared*).	Are we gonna go to Hell?
S.A.	Well, hopefully not. That's why you're gonna need to receive communion.
ERIC CARTMAN.	And as long as we get this communion thing, we're safe?
STAN.	What if we haven't really done anything that horribly bad in our lives?
E.C.	Yeah, what *if* we hadn't?
S.A.	It doesn't matter, because we are all born with original sin. (*Taking plate out.*) Now let me explain how communion works. The priest will give you this round cracker, and he will say, 'The body of Christ.' And then you eat it.
E.C. (*puzzled*).	Jesus was made of crackers?
S.A.	No . . .
STAN.	But crackers are his body.
S.A.	Yes.
KENNY (*muffled*).	What?
S.A.	In the Book of Mark, Jesus distributed bread and said: 'Eat this, for this is my body.'

E.C.	So we won't go to Hell, as long as we eat crackers?
S.A.	No, no, no, no!
BUTTERS.	Well, what are we eatin' then?
S.A.	The body of Christ!
STAN.	No, no, no, I get it. Jesus wanted us to eat him, but he didn't want us to be cannibals, so he turned himself into crackers and then told people to eat 'im.
S.A.	No!
STAN (*desperate*).	No?
BUTTERS.	I can't whistle if I eat too many crackers.
S.A.	Look, all you have to know is that when the priest gives you the cracker, you eat it, OK?
ALL (*dubious*).	O . . . K.
S.A.	And then, you will drink a very small amount of wine. For that is the blood of Christ.
E.C.	Oh come on now, this is just getting silly.[1]
S.A.	Eric, do you want to go to Hell?
E.C.	No![2]

Stan's comment about cannibalism comes like a gunshot out of the comic murk, because it verges so closely on a truth of this deconstructive moment. In this passage from the animated television series *South Park*, nervous Catholic children grapple with the meanings of their inherited faith. Their struggle recapitulates some difficulties of church doctrine.

That the characters of *South Park* are obnoxious cartoon children does not undercut the seriousness of this hilarity: if communion cannot be made to make sense without the threat of eternal torment ratifying it, and without the spectre of cannibalism stalking it, then it is a ritual with an interpretive destiny every bit as problematic as its history. And in the spirit of a comedy about a tragedy, I offer a discussion of *Titus Andronicus*, a tragedy about a comedy.

Claims of Shakespeare's Catholic sympathies could do with some adjustment when it comes to this play. Two separate elements speak against such sympathies. The first is the general association of the play's lunatic tragic hero with the Catholic faith: Titus acts like a priest, presides over funeral rituals (complete with incense); he mortifies his flesh, too eagerly cutting off his own hand, not in an attempt to follow Christ's Sermon on the Mount ('If thy right hand offend thee, cut him off and cast him from thee' – Matthew 5.30), but to save his sons; and he claims he can read his daughter's 'martyr'd signs' after she has been horribly disfigured by his enemies. (The attention to martyrdom per se bespeaks neither Catholic nor Protestant sympathies at this moment in the play; both sects created many a martyr for their rivals' cause.) The second possibly anti-Catholic element, however, offers a more compelling insight into the problem of Shakespeare's belief or unbelief.

The comedy that the play makes into tragedy is the comedy of communion itself. The Last Supper is parodied, made gristly through a banquet sequence that concludes the play. In *Titus Andronicus*, that meal importantly recounts elements of the Eucharist, including the pivotal claim about the real presence of Christ, the very question to which Sister Anne responds so awkwardly for the *South Park* children.

Since one central difference between reform and Catholic theology has to do with that presence, let us consider Titus's gloriously gory banquet. Before we do, let us remember how that meal comes about.

Titus, returned to Rome from his long wars with the Goths, begins the play by performing rites for his newly dead sons. His oldest son, Lucius, helpfully suggests that they perform a human sacrifice to propitiate the gods. He chooses the 'eldest son of this distressed queen' (1.1.103), Alarbus, son of the captive Goth queen Tamora. Despite her pleas, Lucius exits with the victim ('Let's hew his limbs till they be clean consum'd'), and soon re-enters to put a period on the ritual: 'Alarbus' limbs are lopp'd | And entrails feed the sacrificing fire, | Whose smoke like incense doth perfume the sky' (1.1.146–8). Tamora's horrified response – 'O cruel irreligious piety!' (130) – expresses the play's skepticism about the moral worth of sacred ritual. The sacrificing fire has, we can be sure, nothing to do with the gods. And Titus's sacrificial act of appeasement back-fires hugely. For the dissection of Alarbus summons from Tamora, her lover Aaron, and her surviving sons a series of grimly physical retributions which become the plot of the play. Yet even the final turbulence carries overtones of twisted sacrality. In a capstone counter-revenge sequence, Titus kills and grinds up Tamora's sons and serves them up to her, baked in a pie at a formal banquet. Then chaos floods the stage: just after the meal has begun, Titus murders his daughter Lavinia (who has been raped, dismembered, and de-tongued by Tamora's sons); he reveals to the appalled guests their casserole's mystery meat; he stabs Tamora and is slain by the emperor Saturninus, who in turn dies at Lucius's hands.

Nearly everything that happens in *Titus Andronicus* arises from the propitiatory violence of the opening sacrifice, which incurs awful revenges and calls down increasingly spectacular sacrifices. This trend – savagery devolving from religious ritual – culminates in the apparent dismemberment, denaturing, and consumption of human flesh, Tamora's crusty sons.

If Titus is himself priestly in action, other cues suggest that the Andronici are also Catholic-coded in their beliefs. Aaron, for instance, characterizes Lucius thus:

> . . . I know thou art religious,
> And hast a thing within thee called conscience,
> With twenty popish tricks and ceremonies,
> Which I have seen thee careful to observe . . .
>
> (5.1.74–7)

The great general and his family represent an outmoded, a popish dispensation. That Aaron conflates 'conscience' here with 'tricks and ceremonies' seems a convincing critique, if not of Catholicism, then at least of the Andronici. They can be viewed anachronistically as the violent Catholic past of Henrician and Marian England. It would seem, too, that as an encoded Catholic, Titus regards his adversaries as Protestants. When he is about to murder Tamora's sons, he momentarily considers offering them the chance to justify themselves, but thinks better of it: 'What would you say if I should let you speak? | Villains, for shame you could not beg for grace. | Hark, wretches, how I mean to martyr you' (5.2.178–80). Presumably, Protestants would not beg for grace (as it comes by faith alone), which Titus seems to recognize. When the sacrificial moment arrives, Titus asks his daughter to hold the basin that catches their vital fluid: 'Lavinia, come, | Receive the blood' (5.2.196–7), reminiscent of the priest's words in communion ('Take this all of you and drink from it. | This is the cup of my blood'); thus when a moment later he says, 'when that they are dead, | Let me go grind their bones to powder small, | . . . And in that paste let their vile heads be bak'd. | Come, come, be everyone officious | To make this banquet' (5.2.197–202), he summons, as the cartoon character Stan does too, a venerable critique: transubstantiation depends on and narrowly evades the act of cannibalism.

The Eucharist controversy wheeled around the question of metaphor: Is Christ *physically* or *figurally* present in the wafer and wine? The question implies a host of others, which I shall not reproduce here. But if Christ is miraculously, bodily present at the moment of the ingestion of the wafer, then the sacrament ceases to be a referential *sign*, and becomes instead a material fact. Protestants had harsh words about the doctrine that deposited Christ physically in the host: John Bridges, Dean of Salisbury, said Catholics 'turned Chryst out of his owne likenesse, and made him looke lyke a rounde cake, nothyng lyke to Iesus Christe . . . but all is visoured and disguysed under the fourme of a wafer. . . . O blessed GOD, dare they thus disfigure our Lord and Saviour Iesus Christ, or can they make suche a strange metamorphosis of the sonne of God?'[3]

Or: dare they make Him into crackers? Adherents of Christ's material presence in the Eucharist had also to answer (or deflect, with ridicule) the stercoranists, those who took seriously the possibility of Christ's body being not only masticated, but excreted, subject to all cloacal indignities.[4]

The question of consumption and cannibalism in the Christian ritual haunts *Titus Andronicus*. When Titus emulates the sacrament to make martyr pie, he exposes the violence that undergirds all attempts at transcendence, all erasures of the border between human and god, and all attempts to deploy such erasures for vengeance and gain. His act replicates not merely the holy meal, but the controversy around the meal.

For when Titus bellows in triumph about the real presence of Tamora's sons in the dish before them, we can detect his gesture as at once theologically sound and utterly deranged: 'Why, there they are, both baked in this pie; | Whereof their mother daintily hath fed, | Eating the flesh that she herself hath bred. | Tis true, 'tis true . . .' (5.3.60–3). For a terrible moment we are back in Antioch, witnessing with Pericles an incest drama that has strangely become a dining experience. But Titus has no interest in such a secret family affair. Instead, he openly asserts religious revelation, the truth that an audience can only suspect – the material presence of the transformed, unrecognizable body. He does so just after performing a public sacrifice of his own, killing his daughter, then at once disturbingly bidding the guests, in absence of a clear referent: 'Will't please you eat? will't please your highness feed?' (5.3.54). Does he mean them – sacramentally – to consume his daughter, too? While such an outcome seems unthinkable, the great general has specialized in contaminating the sacred ever since he sponsored the ritual killing that fires up the play.

In his confession about the body and blood in the meal, Titus performs a mad, just-off-center misreading of Catholic theology, redeemed (as he thinks) by grotesque sacrificial murder. We see him asymptotically approach an idea of holiness, but it is an idea that doubles for crazed savagery. The mercy killing of Lavinia crystallizes his particular pathology. Perhaps we are meant to recall a similarly appalling sacrifice of God's beloved child. Just as the parodic communion Titus serves to and of his enemies neutralizes yet uncomfortably recalls Christian Eucharistic meanings, so too does the murder of docile Lavinia – not so much as a bleat out of her lamblike self – summon, and reduce to cartoonish informality, the foundational child murder of Christianity. It may be that only those definitively outside the dispensation can react properly to this brand of sickness, this child sacrifice; Saturninus exclaims, aghast: 'What hast thou done, unnatural and unkind?' (5.3.48).

Titus Andronicus stands against sacrifice, a rebuke against the Eucharist ritual. In its relentlessly gory impulse to dismember undergirding structures of thought – and to expose those structures as violent, disintegrative – it causes other forms of violence to manifest themselves. The things that make this play among the most reviled and dismissed in the canon also make it profound, challenging, referential. Perhaps philosophically or ideologically, we demur because our doubts and insecurities are such sensitive instruments: push against them, we spasm. A queasy recognition implicates us in holy violence. The play has simply been waiting for its atheist moment.

Some in Shakespeare's audience may have found it hard to distinguish between Titus the successful revenger and Titus the Catholic/psychotic, yet the play slaps hard at not merely Catholic creed but *any* belief that attempts to valorize the vanquishing of enemies in the name of the holy. Titus claims a real presence, but he cannot see and does not claim the Real Presence of Christ. It seems that Shakespeare cannot see it either.

Any Catholic sympathies in the play, vestiges of a flesh-based faith, are, in the common parlance, crackers: like the hero, completely loony. Though *Titus* does not translate with neat entirety into an anti-Catholic screed, neither does it, with its horrific literalism and dismal martyrdoms, plausibly endorse any faith. As we shall see, only Aaron, the lone major character absent from the unholy meal of the Andronici, rises above the derangements of belief.

In a later, dazzling *South Park* episode,[5] Cartman, the most skeptical of the children about the Lord's Supper – but the one who subsequently finds Mel Gibson's thrashfest *The Passion of the Christ*[6] wildly exciting – puts his religious tuition to good use. He exacts revenge on a rival, a boy named Scott, by arranging for Scott's parents to be killed and served in a bowl of chili. When the mortified boy discovers what he has eaten, Cartman celebrates: 'Nyeah-nyeah nyeah-nyeah nyeah-nyeah, nyeah, I made you eat your parents.' To which his friend Stan responds, even more aptly than Saturninus at Titus's sacrifice of Lavinia: 'Jesus Christ, dude!'

Exactly. But Cartman knows that celebration is only part of the meal, that holy feast memorializes a somber occasion, and so he says to his rival: 'Let me taste your tears, Scott . . . your tears are so yummy and sweet. . . . Oh, the tears of unfathomable sadness!' In South Park, as in Titus's Rome, the meal that memorializes divine sacrifice devolves into a godless execution of successful revenge. A new sacrificial meal of tears, perfect occasional fare for the tragedy in communion, becomes food for one.

Part Two

Purgatory

5 Conspicuously Failed Christ Figures Named Antonio

Antonio and others

Characters named Antonio are not the only conspicuously failed Christ figures in Shakespeare's work, but they are the only ones who are also gay.[1]

If a Christ figure provides, through self-sacrifice, an image of salvation for those who believe in him, then it may not be strictly correct to call these figures 'failed.' Just miserably unhappy.

Stuck in comedies where they lack even the palest thread of a sense of humor, these Antonio Christlets are little genre mistakes, redemptive sufferers in need of salvation, homosexuals whose love dooms them and (it could be argued) generates the very same heteroerotic plot that is their demise, their exclusion. The Antonios from *Twelfth Night* and *The Merchant of Venice* suffer passion for the principal male romantic lead; their generosity on his behalf, and their exclusion in the final heterosexual couples scene, are always affecting.

Antonio the pirate in *Twelfth Night* gives money to Sebastian, then is denied three times (twice with demurrals, the third with silence) by male-disguised Viola, Sebastian's twin. As guards are leading Antonio away, he cries that he 'snatch'd one half' of Viola/Sebastian 'out of the jaws of death' and 'Reliev'd him with such sanctity of love' (3.4.360–1) that he can scarcely believe the youth would deny him now. Suggestively, the guard says: 'What's that to us? The time goes by. Away!' (3.4.364), quoting the priests' and elders' indifference to Judas's recantation in Matthew 27.4. Antonio, like the hero of the recently publicized 'Gospel of Judas,' is sinned against, not sinning: the scout of salvation.

Bassanio owes his friend in *The Merchant of Venice* the same thing Sebastian owes his in Illyria: money and love. (And, like Illyria's 'notable pirate, thou salt-water thief' (5.1.68), the merchant of Venice bases much of his income on venture, ships, and a kind of piracy.) Unlike the virtuous pirate, however, the Venetian Antonio is only too happy to assume the mantle of Sacrificer for Love, and to bastinado his friends with that status. As he awaits the fulfillment of Shylock's contract, he fends off Bassanio's words of comfort: 'I am a tainted wether of the flock, | Meetest for death' (4.1.115–16). His evident eagerness to die cannot be pried from his emotional lock on Bassanio, his debtor: he wishes to repeat Christ's strategy of incurring infinite debt by offering an unanswerable sacrifice.

Does Shakespeare suggest that emotional extortion is part of the Christ model? Does he recall Christopher Marlowe's 'quip about a homoerotic Jesus'?[2] Or is his point more general: that self-identified Christians and Christ figures always fail badly, cannot live up to their own beliefs, or produce misery for others? It is difficult not to conclude with Oscar Wilde, in his astonishing parable 'The Doer of Good,' that even a well-intentioned Christ may have sprung some poorly trained disciples:

And when He had passed through the hall of chalcedony and the hall of jasper, and reached the long hall of feasting, He saw lying on a couch of sea-purple one whose hair was crowned with red roses and whose lips were red with wine.

And He went behind him and touched him on the shoulder and said to him, 'Why do you live like this?'

And the young man turned round and recognized Him, and

made answer and said, 'But I was a leper once, and you healed me. How else should I live?'[3]

Through not always lucid self-interpretation, Jesus finds himself with insufficiently alert believers, the kind who populate the Republican Party in the USA or the Christian community in Shakespeare's Venice. But from another, skeptical perspective, Christ's knowledge of his divinity and his immortality may seem to undermine the grandeur of the gift he gives, or rather keeps: his life. To the extent that Christ has perfect knowledge of his godly origins and his reign in the afterlife, how is his 'sacrifice' anything other than a jumping-the-gun, an early checkout time? Or worse: a spur to the undecided, a guilt-inducing rhetorical shove? The story of his offering can seem, from outside the tradition, rather a peculiar narrative, a self-undoing parable. He who stands as an archetype to believers as the greatest sufferer in history has an insufferability about him, especially to those whose agonies are genuine, prolonged and exploited, terminal, meaningless, and unredeemed by the chance of apotheosis. Now, sharing and helping to bestow eternal life: that's very nice. But that is precisely what Christ *figures* such as Antonio cannot offer; all he can give is eternal guilt. Venetian Antonio represents the extortion of belief inherent in the Christ fable, in that he offers to forgive Bassanio's monetary debt, even as his sacrifice brings (or would bring) a deeper, more destructive, perpetual owing: 'I gave my life for you. Oh, say hi to Portia for me:'

> Commend me to your honorable wife,
> Tell her the process of Antonio's end,
> Say how I lov'd you, speak me fair in death;
> And when the tale is told, bid her be judge
> Whether Bassanio had not once a love.
> Repent but you that you shall lose your friend,
> And he repents not that he pays your debt.

(4.1.273–9)

The debt/death pun performs the Christ figuration: Antonio is pay-ing Bassanio's death, allowing him a new lease on life.

This emotional, Christian chokehold is sly and stunning. Oddly, the hold must be broken, the sacrificial model rejected. Portia, deft Christian that she is, bestows 'life and living' (5.1.286) on Antonio in the end, miraculously canceling his debt. Of course, she thus inflicts real and prolonged suffering on him, for his preferred iden-tification as sacrifice is now convincing only in erotic terms.

'If it's dying and you don't know what it is, it's a Christ figure,' goes a cheeky adage from my early literary tutelage. Truth lurks behind the laugh line: *if you don't know what it is*. *The Merchant of Venice* renders brilliantly the peculiarity of Christian sacrifice: it is not sacrifice at all. You cannot pretend to give graciously that which you can never lose. (Thus Portia, who actually says 'I stand for sacrifice' (3.2.57), projects a 'generosity' and charm that are limited, precisely because her resources are not.) A great debt should be difficult to pay. To claim that your suffering is vast, as Venetian Antonio does, to seize the cov-eted and useful mantle of the Christ figure, is to claim an unimpeachable pain. But Antonio, dreadful Christian, inflicts much greater pain than he suffers. He wreaks this dreadful revenge on the Jew who would not forgive his debt: Antonio makes him live, and live in a religion he cannot but regard as a torment. Antonio knows, as Angelo did, that at a certain point, death is a mercy, the gracious gift. Oscar Wilde again, from the end of the parable:

> And when He had passed out of the city He saw seated by the roadside a young man who was weeping.
>
> And He went towards him and touched the long locks of his hair and said to him, 'Why are you weeping?'
>
> And the young man looked up and recognized Him and made answer, 'But I was dead once and you raised me from the dead. What else should I do but weep?'[4]

Portia punishes Antonio by making him live, denying him the lie of Christ-figuring.

One might wonder if Shakespeare even takes the *figura Christi* seriously. Does anything positive ever come from the Christs on the scaffold?

Yes: theatrical surprise. I'd like to consider some out-of-the-ordinary types of Christ whose attributes mark them as especially troubling, distant from an ordinary inkling of the sacred.

You don't have to be gay and Antonio to be a disappointed Christlike failure in Shakespeare; you simply have to be a sacrificial sufferer who meets and distributes a sorry fate. Cordelia, in *King Lear*, offers the best example. She is supposedly one 'Who redeems nature from the general curse | Which twain have brought her to' (4.6.206–7) – the classic definition of Christ's repair of Adam and Eve's bungled job. And she herself says: 'O dear father, | It is thy business that I go about' (4.4. 23–4), quoting Jesus' own childhood query, 'Know ye not that I must go about my father's business?' (Luke 2.49). So, there you have her: Christ figure. But although she's 'a soul in bliss' (4.7.45), she remains fully unable to redeem her father, whom even she calls 'poor perdu' (4.7.34) – lost sentry, doomed soul. Cordelia not only fails spectacularly, and makes the end of Lear's life heartcrackingly intolerable, but also becomes the subject of an outrageous, accidental jest; Albany actually *loses track of her*: 'Great thing of us forgot! | Speak, Edmund, where's the King? and where's Cordelia?' (5.3.237–8). The loudest 'oops' in Shakespeare, these lines grant Cordelia all the dignity of a pet abandoned in a kennel.

Other Shakespearean Christ figures die without our knowing what they are, in a state of unintelligibility. In *Othello*, we might process in several ways the fact that Desdemona, after having been smothered by her husband, pops back up again as if she'd merely been anaesthetized, not killed; she returns to life so as to attempt a salvational lie:

DESDEMONA.   A guiltless death I die.
EMILIA.   O, who hath done this deed?
DESDEMONA.   Nobody; I myself. Farewell!
                       . . .

OTHELLO.   She's like a liar gone to burning hell:
                  'Twas I that kill'd her.

(5.2.122–30, passim)

However, there's nothing at all redemptive about this lie; indeed, it makes things worse: Othello's vicious response only further clinches his reprobation. Desdemona has been the controlling religious-worship object throughout the play, so her brief bounce-back from death and her well-intentioned attempt to save Othello are not, in some ways, surprising; neither are they helpful, successful, or heartening. But the truly odd choice for Christ figure in the play is none other than the tool, dupe, loser, the one figure in the play (other than Iago) whom we might think lodges furthest from Christian heroism:

CASSIO.   There is besides, in Roderigo's letter,
                  How he upbraids Iago, that he made him
                  Brave me upon the watch...
                              ... and even but now he spake
                  (After long seeming dead) Iago hurt him,
                  Iago set him on.

(5.2.324–9)

The report about Roderigo – dead, revived, dead again – has little practical impact on the denouement. Cassio serves up superfluous information. But Iago's 'purse,' Roderigo, who spoke 'even but now,' might be saved by his stylized death. Does miserable Roderigo now have a sacred, redemptive value by reason of his miraculous, past-last-gasp, stool-pigeoning of Iago? Can it save the soul to betray the devil?

The strangest figure of Christ by far must be among the worst, the most gratuitous, whose resemblance to the redeemer has no taste of suffering, sacrifice, or salvation. Indeed, the oddest such figure in Shakespeare achieves his rank merely through his intermediary position. The young courtier Troilus, in the throes of erotic frustration (which he is ever concerned to transmogrify into something noble), points out his limited courtship options:

> I cannot come to Cressid but by Pandar.
>
> *(Troilus and Cressida,* 1.1.95)

'Jesus saith unto him, I am the way, the truth, and the life: no man cometh unto the Father, but by me' (John 14.6). In rephrasing Jesus' exclusionary statement of salvation, Shakespeare places none other than Pandarus the pimp in the Christ position, the guarantor of blessedness.

Shakespeare's deployment of the dominant religious myth of his day suggests a frayed connection to belief. If Pandarus can take the place of Christ, even syntactically, then holy representations are in trouble. And even when the Christ figure can do the job, as Troy's go-between can, it is scarcely a job that should be done.

6 The Profit-Driven Life

Portia

On one hand, she would likely have received the money had she been a Muslim or a Jew; let me admit as much. But, on the other, she might never have survived her ordeal were she not a Christian, and a resourceful one. Ashley Smith, 26, a widowed single mother from Georgia, pulled off the neatest trick since Portia in *The Merchant of Venice*: she managed financial profit by using Christianity to forestall criminality.

On March 12, 2005, Ms. Smith was taken hostage for 13 hours by a murderer, a man named Brian Nichols, who had killed a judge and three other people, and had escaped the law. But she convinced him, through the force of her character and 'faith,' no doubt – and by reading to him from the pop-spiritual book, Rick Warren's *The Purpose-Driven Life* – that he, a killer, was a person of value, worthy of being tested (and perhaps saved) by God. She persuaded him not merely to let her go, but to turn himself in. The story was a *cause célèbre* for a month. While I have no reason to question Smith's sincerity or the brilliance of her strategy, one fact simply shouts in the aftermath: her triumph earned her about $70,000 (£38,250), the reward money for the fugitive's capture. Praise the Lord for her reward, shouted the religious publications and websites.[1]

Who would be so stingy as to begrudge her money for the successful, pragmatic deployment of her faith in this instance? We know that Warren, whose book provided the getaway manual, would not. But Christ might. Shakespeare almost certainly. Because at the heart of *The Merchant of Venice* lies something that Ms. Smith happily learned and what most politicians, Portia, and Shylock (to his vexation) know: Christianity can be put to use. It is a lever for transcendence or survival; a bludgeon for profit and social mobility; a pillow to muffle the voices of contrary ideologies. Ashley Smith is no Portia; the quality of her mercy was under the severest strain. (Portia never sweats, and, unlike Antonio or Ms. Smith, she never faces the knife.) But like the Venetian Christians, she found a way, through her faith, perhaps her cunning, to profit from her crisis and bring a reprobate to justice. A good day's work.

*　*　*　*　*　*　*　*

Postscript: A second fact shouted even louder in the aftermath of the event. Ms. Smith, as it happened, may not have been quite as seamlessly virtuous as news reports first indicated. In part to pacify, perhaps bribe her captor, Smith admitted to offering him part of her stash of crystal methamphetamine. Far from showing, as one sanctimonious commentator would have it, 'genuine Christian love,' and turning the killer 'from a beast to a brother in Christ,'[2] she may have used the magical powers of modern chemistry to quell or divert his murderous impulses. Such alchemy is not necessarily irreligious. Even Portia turns her Christian profit with a kind of hypnotic (although not drug-assisted) grace. Ms. Ashley Smith could not have performed her desperate improvisation any better even if she had Belmont's advantaged heroine in mind. All she needed to perfect the imitation of Portia was a disguise – which, we discover, she may have worn after all.

7 Moon Changes

Katherina

Katherina's last clear moments of freedom look like this:

PETRUCHIO.   Good Lord, how bright and goodly shines the moon!

KATHERINA.   The moon! The sun – it is not moonlight now.

PETRUCHIO.   I say it is the moon that shines so bright.

KATHERINA.   I know it is the sun that shines so bright.

PETRUCHIO.   Now, by my mother's son, and that's myself,
It shall be moon, or star, or what I list . . .
Evermore cross'd and cross'd, nothing but cross'd!

(The Taming of the Shrew 4.5.2–10, passim)

In Katherina's transformation from 'curst' (as she in her 'shrewish-ness' is often called) to blessed by her new lord, Petruchio, an allegory of forced conversion unfolds. What makes *The Taming of the Shrew* arguably comic rather than tragic, however, is that the compelled belief is mitigated by the convert's own craft. True, the change begins in the manner of a cult brainwashing: Petruchio starves her, deprives her of sleep, embarrasses her to break her spirit. Yet Katherina finds a place to hide, a room in which to keep her personality and creative power intact.

We begin to discern her adaptation to abusive circumstances after the above exchange, one of the most explicitly religious in the play. Still resisting Petruchio's domineering ways, Katherina rejects his arbitrary designation of the real. As the grounds of his own faith

('Now by my mother's son . . .'), Petruchio swears by himself, insisting on the right to dictate significance, to launch a new religion, even if it means switching the names of the two largest heavenly bodies. But in resisting this new world order, Katherina makes Petruchio triply 'cross'd:' maritally, she crosses or disobeys him; ideologically, she frustrates him by subverting his fictional reality; and, spiritually, she deploys the meanings based on the Cross, by asserting that she knows the 'Good Lord,' and the important Son/sun (who is not 'my mother's son') when she sees them. In this last moment of her independence, then, Katherina pledges allegiance to a prior, foundational truth and reality.

Even when Hortensio, with whom the couple is traveling, advises Katherina to 'Say as he says, or we shall never go' (4.5.11), she manages, wittily, to pocket her submission. Petruchio again insists 'I know it is the moon' (4.5.16) and Katherina agrees; he changes his mind, and she pretends religiously to change hers with him: 'Then God be blest, it is the blessed sun. | But sun it is not, when you say it is not; | And the moon changes even as your mind' (4.5.18–20). In this capitulation, Katherina is pragmatic but also shifty: she has just called her husband a lunatic, a moonbat. He hasn't noticed, or does not care as long as he has his way. But momently, she performs an even bolder, if necessarily stealthy, transgression in the guise of obedience.

An old man appears on the road, and, without warning, Petruchio greets him thus: 'Good morrow gentle mistress, where away? | Tell me, sweet Kate, and tell me truly too, | Hast thou beheld a fresher gentlewoman?' (4.5.27–9). Petruchio may expect a hesitant capitulation from Katherina, but she jumps right in with the play's most endearing moment: 'Young budding virgin, fair and fresh, and sweet, | Whither away, or where is thy abode? | Happy the parents of so fair a child!' (4.5.37–9). Not satisfied with this triumph, or maybe sensing her pleasure, Petruchio wants to make Katherina retract her speech, and points out that they are talking to an old man. And she replies:

> Pardon, old father, my mistaking eyes,
> That have been so bedazzled *with the sun*,
> That everything I look on seemeth green.

> (4.5.45–7)

Thus does Katherina, razor sharp, prove Petruchio wrong – it *is* the sun, and not the moon – and thus does she win the argument at the exact moment when she pretends to submit to her husband's position.

The fact that she can find small, clever victories in the midst of her submission does not excuse Petruchio's self-conscious savagery. Some of his cruelty has a specifically spiritual cast to it. For instance, his first conjugal move – walloping the priest at the wedding cere-mony – proves vital. An attack on the sanctity and indeed the untouchability of other systems of belief is the first step towards establishing a new system: when the priest asks if Petruchio would take Katherina as his wife, '"Ay, by goggs wouns," quoth he, and swore so loud, | That, all amaz'd, the priest let fall the book, | And as he stoop'd again to take it up, | This mad-brain'd bridegroom took him such a cuff | That down fell priest and book, and book and priest' (3.2.160–4). Priest, book: two crucial vehicles of God's grace, and Petruchio attacks them. The strategic assault makes a joke of holy oaths, and replaces reverence with fear. Petruchio plays the terrorist here, strategically deploying religious violence to pro-duce public horror. He gives the impression that there is nothing he would not try. Later, we find out what he's been thinking:

> Nay, I will win my wager better yet,
> And show more sign of her obedience,
> Her new-built virtue and obedience.

> (5.2.116–18)

He knows the only necessary and sufficient prerequisite of religion: obedience. Katherina's new-built virtue *is* obedience.

Yet we've seen that Katherina complicates, at least for a time, the obedience question, and, in so doing, she undercuts such religion as

Petruchio imagines he's established. Her father imagines her newly made – 'For she is chang'd, as she had never been' (5.2.112–15) – but he is an untrustworthy reader in such matters. Katherina's belief has a purgatorial undecidability about it: we never hear her in soliloquy, and thus it becomes difficult to chart her on the spiritual grid. To assess her new faith, we must rely on her tour de force, public performance: the over-the-top lambasting she gives the fractious women at the end of the play for their casual spousal disobedience. Surely, in scourging the women for insufficient submissiveness, Katherina's domineering speech undercuts its own argument. Yes, she's lording it over women, not men, but we see that the impulse to command still reigns in her. Beyond that contradiction, something important, foundational, goes wrong in that final speech, that ode to the proper wifely view of the world. Something goes missing.

Love, of course. Her utterance trumpets her duty, but in that 43-line coming-out, love is only mentioned twice. And when it is spoken, it cannot escape the magnetic field of Petruchio's favorite word. One's husband, Katherina says,

> . . . craves no other tribute at thy hands
> But love, fair looks, and true obedience.
>
> (5.2.152–3)

If love and fair looks sound like reasonable accompaniments to true obedience, the orthodox patriarchal position returns with a harder edge when she says, just 12 lines later, that women should never seek 'rule, supremacy, and sway, | When they are bound to serve, love, and obey' (163–4). Love has now sidled up to obedience, trapped or bound irretrievably in the line between 'serve' and 'obey.' As she rails at the Widow and Bianca, Katherina speaks of the husband-function as mainly protective; her metaphors pitch towards military and state, not God or family. And they certainly dodge the erotic and romantic.

Katherina's center-stage triumph obscures the convert's humility and the message of faith. Which must, if nothing else, be the message of love. For faith remains questionable where love slavishly mimes obedience. But she now lacks any other model for belief. Her conversion is doubtful, particularly because her speech about wifely duty goes out of its way *not* to describe Petruchio; nor does it compare her lord to her Lord, as the similar speech in the source/analogue play (*The Taming of A Shrew*) does. We simply cannot be certain, that is, about Katherina's commitment to belief.

This, after all, is the crux of any conversion: if you do not stand where you are because of love, your bond is merely submission, or, at best, accommodation. Katherina may take pleasure, have joy, in her triumph over other women. She may even share a brief conjugal moment that looks (but is not so) tender, the 'kiss me, Kate' exchange (5.1.143ff.): here Petruchio orders a kiss, she shyly refuses, he turns to leave, and, once again compelled, she capitulates with the smooch and the supplication ('Now pray thee, love, stay') that wins her wish. But her pleasures, however she finds them, never give what she and we crave: signs of *mutual* and uncoerced obedience to a thought of love, by which trials might be redeemed.

Katherina's bid for independence closed with her confession to having been dazzled by the sun. Sadly, that seems correct. The sun, after all, need not obey the moon. And the moon only shines through the sun's good graces.

8 Happy Suicide

Hamlet

The question seems settled early on: he wishes 'that the Everlasting had not fix'd | His canon 'gainst self-slaughter! O God, God,' Hamlet laments (*Hamlet*, 1.2.131–2). Punning with aplomb, he hopes that his sullied/sallied flesh would 'melt, | Thaw, and resolve itself into a dew,' or adieu. 'A-dieu:' 'to God.' It seems as if the presence of the divine and his prohibitions against suicide are fairly secure, even if Hamlet does wish to go to God, without further ado. Later, when the Ghost says 'Adieu, adieu, adieu!, remember me' (1.5.91), it seems as though Hamlet already has, even before the spirit shows up: his terrors melt, thaw, and resolve themselves into the Ghost of his father, bidding him goodbye.

But God's 'canon' against suicide, a general prohibition against the spiritual crime of despair, might also be a 'cannon' the Almighty fixes against those who would rob Him of divine prerogative. Taking aim against any who would try to control the terms of their own death, God has special punishments in store for the jaunty – or, like Ophelia, the oblivious – slaughterers of themselves.

The question of Ophelia's suicide draws witty interrogation from the gravediggers: 'Is she to be buried in Christian burial when she willfully seeks her own salvation?' (5.1.1–2). Where *is* the sin in seeking one's own salvation? We might wish also to know how anyone could think this was suicide when we have Gertrude's excruciating, slow-motion, eyewitness account of the drowning. Ophelia's poetic demise, however, brings up more extensive issues than Gertrude's passive perfidy.

Ophelia, like her brother, draws her chief significances (sad to say) as a Hamlet-displacement: Shakespeare mostly cares about her insofar as she illuminates, focuses, and reduces crises that the prince endures. This question of suicide, however, is keen, and one where Ophelia actually expands or magnifies something 'doubtful' about Hamlet: his suicidal and therefore damnable end.

He had been thinking about it since his first soliloquy. And the question undergirds the 'To be or not to be' speech, whether or not we read the famous lines that way (and Douglas Bruster rightly cautions us not to restrict their meanings thus).[1] But the question of suicide shadows other elements in the play, including Ophelia's fate. We have Hamlet's obscure warning to his mother not 'To try conclusions in the basket creep | And break your own neck down' (3.4.195–6); there is his brinksmanship in the Gonzago playlet, guaranteed to draw Claudius's ire, and his fire; and we hear Hamlet's envious regard of Fortinbras, who seems carelessly to be risking his life for a trifle of worthless ground, 'Exposing what is mortal and unsure | To all that fortune, death, and danger dare, | Even for an egg-shell' (4.4.51–3). No doubt: he has suicide envy.

Lucky for him that he eventually gets the chance to put on heroism, as a 'compell'd valor' (4.6.18): in fights against pirates, Laertes in the grave, and Laertes/Claudius in the court. Lucky too that that last fight causes his friend Horatio, 'more an antique Roman than a Dane' (5.2.341), to profess his own suicidal impulse to follow the slain prince. But most fortunate of all is the way Hamlet fulfills his long-held desire 'to melt, thaw,' without the stigma of suicide attached. For self-murder surely describes his end. His own acceptance of Laertes' obvious sword fight set-up tells us that he knows and welcomes what is coming: 'Thou wouldst not think how ill all's here about my heart – but it is no matter' (5.2.212–3). He then delivers his famous 'readiness is all' nugget, indicating a stoic resolve to die when the time comes, because now he is in God's hands.

This opportunistic abandonment to someone else's plot – effectively Claudius's, supposedly God's, but really Hamlet's – has all the earmarks of 'bullshit,' as Harry Frankfurt defines the term:

> It does seem that bullshitting involves a kind of bluff. It is closer to bluffing, surely, than to telling a lie. . . . Unlike plain lying, however, [bluffing] is more especially a matter not of falsity but of fakery. This is what accounts for its nearness to bullshit. For the essence of bullshit is not that it is *false* but that it is *phony*. . . . [The bullshitter's] only indispensably distinctive characteristic is that in a certain way he misrepresents what he is up to. . . . The bullshitter. . . . does not reject the authority of the truth, as the liar does, and oppose himself to it. He pays no attention to it at all. By virtue of this, bullshit is a greater enemy of the truth than lies are.[2]

We might pause for a moment and consider the usefulness of Frankfurt's categories to a description of ideology in general, and religion in particular.

Frankfurt's sharp rhetorical description explains the prince's urge to describe his work in the world as God's labor. He has been so convinced by the canon against self-slaughter that he has used his capacious brain to bluff a way around it, and the best way he can find is through God's own plan: 'if it be not now, yet it will come' (5.2.221). Yes, yes, but he can help 'it' along. And so he does.

Hamlet's arc can be traced convincingly from rejection to acceptance of suicide. In bullshitting his way into the God zone – where even in helping kill Rosencrantz and Guildenstern without 'shriving time allow'd' (5.2.47) he finds 'heaven ordinant' – Hamlet replicates one of the more ignoble causes of religious fervor: to justify almost any self-serving deed. He cannot see, and thus effectively shields, his own implication in the ruin of an entire kingdom which falls *by reason of his de facto suicide*, his agreeing to the rigged swordfight with Laertes. Hamlet knows he is swiftly headed towards death. That suits him fine, and it always has.

Maybe, to give him his due, Hamlet seeks to die as a way to fulfill or cure, in Ewan Fernie's words, his own 'sophisticated sense of shame and what is degrading.'[3] Hamlet has ample cause for the feeling. In the anthology of the unseemly and embarrassing that he constructs, no more revealing moment appears than the fight over Ophelia's corpse. This pageant of grief is so false and imitative that we could not imagine either Hamlet or Laertes would long survive the shame. But enfolded in the humiliating act is a weird religious aspiration:

> HAMLET.   Dost thou come here to whine?
> To outface me with leaping in her grave?
> Be buried quick with her, and so will I.
> And if thou prate of mountains, let them throw
> Millions of acres on us, till our ground,
> Singeing his pate against the burning zone,
> Make Ossa like a wart!
>
> (5.1.277–83)

Both Hamlet and Laertes wish to emulate the Titans, who tried to heap mountain on mountain until they reached heaven. In some exceedingly strange way, Hamlet and Laertes conceive their stagey grief as a model of purgatory, a mountainous stepladder to transcendence. Do they really think that the construction of a super-hill on the body of Ophelia will bring them closer to heaven? It is a marvelous vignette of shame, self-justification, and rampant bullshit.

Hamlet does have his instances of grace. 'And when you are desirous to be blest | I'll blessing beg of you' (3.4.171–2), he says in a glimpse of gentleness to his mother. He shows kindness and respect to the players, who could certainly use it. He speaks to a traumatized Ophelia (after he's traumatized her) the disarmingly self-critical 'What should such fellows as I do crawling between earth and heaven?' (3.1.126–8). He offers stoic, male-bonding tenderness to Horatio: 'Give me that man | That is not passion's slave, and I will wear him | In my heart's core, ay, in my heart of heart, | As I do thee'

(3.2.71–4). And perhaps most touchingly, he says about Polonius, 'I'll lug the guts into the neighbor room' (3.4.212).

Oh, wait. Who said that? The other Hamlet, clearly, the one Horatio chooses not to remember in his 'flights of angels' prayer. The play labors hard to suggest that its hero is redeemable. In religious terms, as far as Hamlet is concerned, the main threat to his salvation seems to lie in that troublesome desire for suicide – not in any of his countless acts and words of savagery and turpitude. If Hamlet can happily enough deal death to others, which he never seems to regard as a moral problem, then why *should* there be any difficulty with suicide, with his seeking his own salvation? All it takes is a clever reframing of the question, and then, blessedly, the rest is . . .

9 It is Required

Leontes and audience

> Faith is a lullaby, sung to put the soul to sleep.
>
> – Robert Ingersoll[1]

Miracles, whatever their ingredients, make a dreadful recipe for belief. Just as hard or extreme cases form bad law, so the inexplicable, seemingly transcendent event creates a dicey precedent for faith.

Why? If the miracle is false, a fraud or merely a misreading, the believer looks stupid, and the grounds of belief erode. If the wonderful event is amazingly true, the miracle raises more questions than it answers: Where have miracles been until now? Why this image or marvel in this place at this time? Why not something more useful, like the end of all disease? Northrop Frye's discomfort with the Gospels' 'displaying of miracles as irrefutable stunts'[2] speaks to the inauthentic, trivial quality of even a foundational account of miracles. But Western religion would scarcely exist without them.

Miracles ought to pour radiance over the world, or light it up from within, but they illuminate practical more often than supernal doings. Holy manifestations perform work: they stanch a drainage of belief, revitalize hope's wilted flower, galvanize the faithful, win converts to the cause. A great paradox of the religious sensibility is that it should seem so often to require such refreshments. When proof must bolster faith, what exactly pulses belief through the blood? The evidence of things seen.

Some of these things are indeed surprising, and they generate both belief and angry denial.

Chicago, Illinois, Friday, May 6, 2005 – A man was arrested for allegedly scrawling the words 'big lie' over a stain on an expressway underpass that some believed was an image of the Virgin Mary.[3]

The Virgin Mary underpass stain had a compellingly equivocal effect, sparking belief and iconoclasm. Even the author of 'big lie' might be something other than what he seems: not necessarily a committed skeptic or atheist, but maybe a true Protestant believer, enraged at the perceived idolatry of supplication to a smear on cement.

Claims of the miraculous may be illusory or ambivalent, and they can provoke destructive denial (even, some say, crucifixions). The article about the Virgin underpass stain continues:

The stain was likely the result of salt runoff, according to the Illinois Department of Transportation.

Worldwide, people have been drawn to images believed to resemble the Virgin Mary seen on windows, fence posts and walls.

One of the best known was an image on windows of an office building in Clearwater, Florida, that drew hundreds of thousands of viewers after it was spotted in 1996. Experts said the image was created by corrosion. The windows were shattered last year, and a teenage boy pleaded guilty to felony criminal mischief and sentenced to 10 days in jail.

The fragile fate and equivocal nature of the miraculous image paves the way to my argument here, as I mean to question if not efface the reverential response some readers have had to just such an image: the resurrection of Hermione in *The Winter's Tale*.

The surprising Virgin manifestations, like that climactic moment of *The Winter's Tale*, provide a Rorschach test for attitudes to religion or revelation itself. Believers revere or construct what they see; doubters – believers of a different stripe – scoff or strike the image out of existence. Some of the best, most clear-eyed readers of Shakespeare prostrate themselves into a position of credulity at the altar of this play, in a way they do nowhere else. Intimidated by such vehemence, doubting critics tend to skulk around the edges of their own commentary, toe-dipping their skepticism about the 'unconvincing' effects of the brash revival scene and the celebratory business of the play's end. I shall come into the open with my idol-effacing response, but hope to show that Shakespeare's own opulent doubts about the meaning of such resurrections spark a properly godless reply to the play. Coercion and theatrical larceny are the dramatist's tools for pushing his miracle through – and the closer we come to the miraculous, the nearer to pragmatism, excess, and corruption its origins appear.

How to sidestep or cow the destructive scorn of the unbeliever? If an artist wishes to write about belief, but does not want to have 'big lie' written over his work, he/she must operate strategically. Here's how to do it: anticipate unbelief. Stare it down with increasingly absurd dramaturgy and brassy unlikelihood of event and motive. And of course, acknowledge the implausible all the way, from the title (a 'winter's tale' is a mere hearthside yarn, spun to keep away ghosts and goblins) through to the ending:

PAULINA.   That she is living,
                Were it but told you, should be hooted at
                Like an old tale: but it appears she lives . . .

                                    (5.3.115–17)

It also would help to show that marvels cannot be bought on the cheap – doubts, losses, constant sorrows are the price they exact. Reveal, in other words, that belief is difficult, but rewarding, and the balance sheet may seem by the end serenely plausible (or not disturbingly out of whack). However, even with all the apparatus of belief in play, what is interesting about Hermione's quickening, particularly in light of recent Virgin Mary sightings, is the way Shakespeare seems incapable of excluding the skeptical response.

Hermione comes to life, and we may feel brief shock, but as soon as the moment dawns, so does realization:

CAMILLO.   If she pertain to life, let her speak too.
POLIXENES. Ay, and make it manifest where she has liv'd,
            Or how stolen from the dead!

(5.3.113–15)

In wanting to know the nuts-and-bolts process of Hermione's preservation, Polixenes amusingly threatens the magic of the moment. Believers are fortunate the play ends when it does: because to 'make it manifest where she has liv'd' is entirely to explode the miracle of her revival, and expose the machinations of Paulina. And that's where things get messy.

For a desperation clings to the shadows of what Paulina has done. Watching the characters and critics overcome their knowledge of the real is an education in willed submission to belief. Audiences follow Leontes following Paulina's central dictum, as she prepares to bring the statued Hermione to life: 'It is requir'd | You do awake your faith' (5.3.94–5).

*   *   *   *   *   *   *   *

The requirement of belief is the single necessary component of ideology. Propaganda does not convince or argue the subscribers into belief: it presupposes, scares up, or requires mute unreasoning acceptance, and then supports that faith with threats, guilt, myths, jiggered evidence, appeals to shame, love, and anguish. Most of the commentators who praise Shakespeare's art of the miraculous quote Paulina approvingly. But they do not notice the freight of her 'required.' Such a requirement steals the marvelous from miracles. And the passive voice of concealed authority underlines her rhetoric of compulsion: It IS REQUIRED you DO awake. . . . Such enforcement does not have the quality of a colloquial encouragement such as 'you gotta believe.' Instead, this is pure arm-twisting.

Why the requirement? Because there would not be a serious play without it. Belief is compulsory in part to create a holy image on stage, and in part to fend off absurdity: laughable or downright goofy effects would otherwise be exposed. If Leontes' and the audience's faith have been sleeping all this while – for the bulk of the play – then their analytical faculties must be tabled now to allow the business of belief to occur. Faith awakes, reason slumps into a coma. But Paulina and Hermione's scam of the statue could only be a patent absurdity were it not for the injunction to belief.

Paulina is meant to recall St. Paul, as she does for many readers, and the nominal similarity conjures Paul's central notion that faith alone establishes the proper relationship to God – awakened faith is required, that is, for salvation. Such a dictum is particularly important here, because if you instead relied on works, or on the thought of work, you'd have to confront the sweating labor that has indeed gone into the miracle before us. The work, however, does not signify charity, or prayer, or other generous deeds. It is the work of conniving, torturing, withholding, and, yes, the work of suffering required to bring about such happiness as obtains at the play's end.

If 'Faith is the secret of one's conscience . . . made manifest by the good works in which it lives,'[4] then, at least in the Catholic view, works externalize the inner mechanism of faith. What happens at the end of *The Winter's Tale*, then, is truly remarkable from a doctrinal perspective: Shakespeare reverses that inner–outer distinction. In the charged, faux-Catholic tableau of Perdita kneeling to the statue of her sainted mother, and with that statue (as with so many Marian miracles) seeming to come alive, Paulina's requirement to awake your faith is really a demand that you expose or externalize your own credulity. Faith emerges, in the open, and works remain hidden. The faith requirement obscures the elaborate manipulation needed to jack this miracle up off the low road of works. Faith is needed as an *alibi*, not a condition for miracle. The play, and Paulina, have an enormous stake in *not* showing works.

*   *   *   *   *   *   *   *

Leontes never really had a problem with faith, per se. While his insistence on his wife's infidelity betrays his own imaginative faithlessness, it also bespeaks his almost instantaneous commitment to a life-changing idea. Such a quality is, we might say, required for the penitent to credit Hermione's resurrection. The play consequently tracks the pathology of his excessive belief.

Belief, for all its positive effects, can open people up to abuse. One form of such abuse takes the shape of the 'long con,' a confidence game in which a carefully elaborated fiction nets riches through the patient, oblivious complicity of the 'mark.' The victim's perceived intimacy with the game itself allows the duping to succeed, and to become the more dramatic and devastating.

The Winter's Tale performs with humor and subtlety, and real brutality, just such a con. It might be hard to detect the game (and the mark) were it not for an unmissable change in the fourth act of the play: Shakespeare's generous provision of a new character, Autolycus, an interpretive template for questions of fraud and artifice. For in a play seemingly about the restitution, through the aid of faith and art, of things that have been lost, Autolycus presents an image of the artist as unregenerate con man – a deft career pickpocket. In a godless key – he says, 'for the life to come, I sleep out the thought of it' (4.3.30) – this character deploys just such tricks and feints as Hermione and Paulina pretend to put to spiritual ends. He steals money; they steal time.

The parallel between the rogue and the noblewomen should influence a reading of the play. Autolycus's comic excursus on torture (4.4.772–91) takes an especially evocative place in the proceedings. Disguised as a courtier, he delivers a speech to the Old Shepherd and his son, designed to scare them into disclosing their secrets and especially their monies. Autolycus summons a range of torments to which the presumptuous shepherds will be subject unless they come across with the goods he demands: 'He has a son, who shall be flayed alive, then 'nointed over with honey, set on the head of a wasps' nest, then stand till he be three quarters and a dram dead' (783–6). The terrors are merely meant to extract a profit. But, though entertaining in context, the lines prepare us for another scene of richer and more blood-curdling torment. Which arrives very soon:

PAULINA.   If, one by one, you wedded all the world,
               Or, from the all that are, took something good
               To make a perfect woman, she you kill'd
               Would be unparallel'd.

LEONTES.   I think so. Kill'd?
      She I kill'd?

                                         (5.1.13–17)

Can we not envision this Promethean organ-tearing scene played repeatedly over the past 16 years? Autolycus's whimsical torture threat has a serious punchline when the young shepherd says of his botherer: 'We are bless'd in this man, as I may say, even bless'd' (4.4.827–8) – a sentiment that anticipates Leontes' somehow, eventually, feeling *grateful* for the misery that Paulina and Hermione inflict.

Let us not obscure the nature of their work: it is *torture*. And it is crueler than wasps attacking flayed skin. For 16 years Paulina has convinced Leontes that he has killed his wife when she knows that he has, in fact, not. What does it mean that she assaults him thus, and then flays him with 'faith'? Her emotional criminality, complicit with Hermione's, is so much worse than anything he's done in his mad jealousy that it presents an exit strategy for his self-forgiveness. But once he discovers the real wonder of the play – not that his wife is newly alive, but that she has been hiding the whole time – Leontes has his soul's pockets picked clean of illusion and even of his own redeeming guilt.

Imagine the shock to find you've been so horribly duped: Leontes' mad jealousy, with its terrible outcome, has been requited with almost unimaginable, sustained viciousness. Not a promising second start to the marriage. Commentators so infrequently remark on the plot problem here that we must conclude the play's defensive 'it's only a tale' pose somehow works: it rigs a semipermeable membrane for meaning. Wonder and joy can pass through, but the normal reaction to a life-stealing humiliation such as the king has suffered somehow remains, dumbstruck, at the gates.

The miserable state to which Leontes comes at the play's end seems to have been predicted by Antigonus, another doomed figure. About to leave Sicilia, the more-or-less virtuous counselor is soon to take the baby Perdita to near-certain death. But as he shifts his words to the child, they stick to Leontes:

> Sir, be prosperous
> In more than this deed does require! And blessing
> Against this cruelty fight on thy side,
> Poor thing, condemn'd to loss!

(2.3.189–92)

The words to the baby track back to the king, who will certainly require blessing against cruelty, poor thing; his condemnation to loss is far more certain than Perdita's.

Shakespeare's incandescent dramatic poetry at the end of the play makes the critical part of the con, the one that impels belief, extremely hard to defend against. In the presence of such refulgent, glorious words, we can scarcely imagine that the great reanimation scene is merely the coda to a long and filthy trick:

PAULINA.   As she liv'd peerless,
         So her dead likeness, I do well believe,
         Excels what ever yet you look'd upon,
         Or hand of man hath done; therefore I keep it
         Lonely, apart. But here it is; prepare
         To see the life as lively mock'd as ever
         Still sleep mock'd death. Behold, and say 'tis well.

(5.3.14–20)

It *is* well, even exquisite, poetically speaking. But 'mock'd' describes the effect better than Paulina intends. The account she gives of her art betrays her.

* * * * * * * *

Like any good confidence game, *The Winter's Tale* leaves plenty of evidence of its bad faith hidden in plain sight; but it is our hapless desire to believe that plays us false. The young shepherd's sense of having been 'blest' by being abused – not an unfamiliar sentiment in religious spheres – comes as well to the foreground of an audience's feeling after *The Winter's Tale* has ended, particularly if the performance lingers over the interminable pastoral scene and then highlights the extortionate spirituality of the resurrected statue.

Yet even Leontes, doomed flagellant, picks up, at least subconsciously, on Paulina's terms and her work: gazing at Hermione, he says, 'The fixure of her eye has motion in't, | As we are mock'd with art' (5.3.67–8). His dawning awareness of what has happened, the notion that art, idol, or image is at its heart a mockery, sets him on a tightrope above the steep ravine. The play keeps him aloft at the end, teetering on the thin wire of Paulina's required belief. And it is the saving possibility of *sincerity* – that some manner of rebirth has occurred – that keeps the tension in that wire.

For all the available skepticism about false or compelled faith in *The Winter's Tale*, the play features one element that demands consideration as supernatural, if not miraculous, particularly in the context of Leontes' duping. This element controls every moment from Hermione's vanishing to her waking: it is perfectly imaged in the tableau of a statue slowly, stiffly descending. I refer to the almost unbelievable *restraint* that the women had to exercise in order to wait a decade and a half to spring their punishing reward on the abject Leontes. Beyond sadistic, this restraint makes such an effective con (and an especially long one) precisely because it produces torment *in the punishers themselves* at a staggering cost. The profit, in such a game, is zero sum: the price of the con is incalculable, which clinches its effectiveness.

At the end of the play, Hermione tells Perdita that, having learned 'that the oracle | Gave hope thou wast in being, [I] have preserv'd | Myself to see the issue' (5.3.126–8). As this comment undoes – exposes – most of Paulina's faith-based mystifications, potentially producing a backlash from Leontes, Paulina quickly and aggressively interjects: 'There's time enough for that,' and furthers the misdirection with a phony, self-pitying lament about her solitude: 'Go together, | You precious winners all' (5.3.128–31). Her art is indeed highly developed. Shakespeare may identify with Autolycus, the fiction-spinning, scene-stealing artisan who helps bring about happiness against his will, and in the absence of faith. But the rogue, skilled and emotionless, loses out in the end. He's a piker, his skullduggery easily recognizable; Paulina, passionately committed scam artist, and secret worker of agonizing plots, is the pro here. Her superhuman restraint creates the miracle that does not exist: the reanimation of a dead woman who has not died, the coming to life of a statue which was never anything other than flesh. She rigs a con game which somehow manages to satisfy many viewers and, for the time being, Leontes himself. Even fraudulent marvels can, for a time, make believers happy. That's the secret of the con, whether religious, theatrical, or criminal.

Perhaps miracles are merely, purely, texts: open to interpreters' hopes and scorn. On the way to a bookstore recently, I passed a church with a sign in front that said simply 'Jesus is Alive.' The claim, earnest and urgent, could mean so many things: a promise, a threat, a daydream, a celebration, depending on the inclination of the reader. A few weeks later I returned to the bookstore by the same route, and beheld the sign in the same place, but now much changed. A single letter had vanished – blown away by a mischievous wind, stolen by a cad, removed for repair, I could not tell.

The sign now said 'Jesus is Ali e.' Miracles of meaning can come by disappearances too, thefts, or subtractions: for the disappointed, or the newly, strangely hopeful, a form of revelation.

10 A Winter's Fable

Lear

Once, long ago, lived a man who was only ever old.

From his earliest years, his passions pitched him towards decrepitude. He grew up mimicking the worst habits of age: hunched-over secrecy, panic about time. Fear clipped his breath. His vision sharpened around coins and food; his ears clogged at mention of his faults.

Did a spell turn him so? No one knew, but malevolent spirits were blamed. Before his mother vanished, she hired a healing Fool to teach him what-for. But motley made no headway with the boy.

He was old before his time, but worse: his passions ran backwards and inside out. Only the things he ought to have hated and instinctively recoiled from found their way into the circle of his care. Tenderly he nursed back to health an adder his dogs had savaged. A rabid mouse knocked about his room, and then his heart; its death struck him hard, hard. And that which most people would love, he could not. Physical comfort meant nothing to him; he lay on pine needles to sleep, lit no fires when cold knotted his lungs. One by one, as reviled things captured his bliss, that which could have adored him slipped away. Soon, nothing in the world was not strange to him.

Then his far-away father died, and the mind-sick boy became king.

He grew up and slept with the wives of his courtiers, and when the unlucky women bore children from the union, hatred grew between bastard sons and betrayed mothers, husbands and wives. The hatred turned on the king, and he absorbed it.

Attempts to kill him failed. Two of his daughters tried several times, in response to which he felt the stirrings of a harsh, peculiar love for them. Something congealed within – stone-cold porridge of pleasure – when he saw his disorders reflected in his children and the court. Those few who shared his malady, who knew the king could never love them, damned themselves to their devotion.

Years lumbered past. In a dream, an immense metallic hand clutched at his throat and pulsed, letting him breathe only in bursts, then cutting off his air. He awoke and called his soothsayer: What does this dream mean? She told him the gods were planning his death, but they meant to torment him first.

He hoped to torment them instead. He would ruin the kingdom that worshipped them. 'I decree,' he said, rolling out the map of the nation, 'that one third of my country will worship only Ronegil, one third will perform rites for Renga, and the dearest third' – here he pointed out those dwelling near the court, in the lush farmlands and orchards – 'will pay homage to Rodeliac.' His lords and courtiers gasped, as if in the grip of a dismal hand.

Fools rhymed him, balladeers sang in anger:

> *Who's the dingle dangle king?*
> *Handy dandy, wretched thing!*
> *Watch him as he splits the ring*
> *And wrecks the universe-o!*
>
> *Thrum and hum the stormy day,*
> *He will never do or say*
> *Anything that's in heart's way,*
> *Stupidly perverse-o!*

His plan worked at once, as chaos descended. 'My illness shall be general. None can resist the division, rivals will demolish one another, and the gods will die when their worshippers do. So am I revenged for this death.'

And as he felt the fires of his life go out, a rot creeping through his chest, he laughed with full-bodied pleasure his strange child's laugh, a testament to wonder.

* * * * * * * *

Galaxies distant, the star monsters noticed a gap in the clay they had made.

Part Three

Heaven

11 Aaron Ascendant

Aaron

Only by contemplating the death of Catholicism is it possible to curb evil in the world.

No, really.

Here is Second Goth, explaining his discovery of the villain of *Titus Andronicus*:

> Renowmed Lucius, from our troops I stray'd
> To gaze upon a ruinous monastery,
> And as I earnestly did fix mine eye
> Upon the wasted building, suddenly
> I heard a child cry underneath a wall.

(5.1.20–4)

It is a compelling moment, a carefully nonpartisan recollection of Catholic ruins in the nation. What is that 'worthy Goth' (as Lucius calls him) thinking, and what exactly captures his attention?

Whatever it is, his contemplative earnestness enables a crucial discovery that helps root out evil: the crying child belongs to Aaron the Moor. The father's overheard soliloquy to the babe, perceptible because of the silence of the monastic ruins, accidentally betrays the atheist villain, who hides amid the wreckage of a religion – anachronistically, Henry VIII's handiwork. Before we know it, the ex-Catholic site has yielded up . . . Satan!

LUCIUS.   O worthy Goth, this is the incarnate devil
          That robb'd Andronicus of his good hand;
          This is the pearl that pleas'd your empress' eye . . .

                                                    (5.1.40–2)

And yet, if the ruined monastery helps in the discovery and purg-
ing of the devil from the play, it also – ambiguously – betrays a
'pearl,' a term long synonymous with Christ. The discovery gives
Shakespeare a chance to toy with shifting identifications of sacred
and profane. Aaron, bribing Lucius to keep the child alive, prom-
ises to show him 'wondrous things, | That highly may advantage
thee to hear' (5.1.55–6), in exchange for Lucius's oath to let the
child live. But the wonders are scarcely miracles; they are, in fact,
horrors: 'For I must talk of murthers, rapes, and massacres, | Acts of
black night, abominable deeds . . .' (5.1.63–4).

Aaron demands an oath from Lucius to preserve his child, yet
Lucius knows that the Moor 'believest no god: | That granted, how
canst thou believe an oath?' (5.1.71–2). Aaron responds that he
does not, in fact, have a religion, but he knows that stooges do, and
he can trust their credulity:

> Yet, for I know thou art religious,
> And hast a thing within thee called conscience,
> With twenty popish tricks and ceremonies,
> Which I have seen thee careful to observe,
> Therefore I urge thy oath; ... I know
> An idiot holds his bauble for a god,
> And keeps the oath which by that god he swears . . .

                                                    (5.1.74–80)

Aaron's professed atheism and scorn of religion – he is the only
Shakespeare character whose godlessness is explicitly announced as
such and is intimately related to his villainy – may illustrate
Montaigne's idea that custom and place are stronger than nature,
and create their own truth.[1] His exotic origins provide something of

an explanation for his intense dislike of 'popish tricks and ceremonies' (thus endearing him to a segment of Shakespeare's
audience?) as well an alibi for his aggressive unbelief. Captured along
with Tamora at the beginning of the play, Aaron remains dedicated
to a revenge against Titus that never makes much sense in terms of
plot, nation, or even personal alliances. But it makes a good deal of
sense as an exposure of false belief, a gloss on 'true' religion.

For Aaron, surprisingly enough, is a pearl, and of great price, too:
an enlightened if concealed holy figure and enemy of hypocrisy. His
job in the play is to test faith, to expose religious fraud, and to perform acts of charity. He asks for Lucius's word not to harm the child,
and then provides a spiritual trial: he offers an account of his crimes
and cruelties so ugly that his words should almost guarantee that
Lucius break the oath. Aaron taunts his captors, expressing regret
that he could not do more evil than he's done, giving us a catalog of
his deeds that includes murder, rape, bearing false witness, setting
fire to barns – bidding 'the owners quench them with their tears' –
harming poor men's livestock, disinterring corpses. That last is a
good one: Aaron set the dead bodies 'upright at their dear friends'
door | Even when their sorrows almost was forgot, | And . . . | Have
with my knife carved in Roman letters | "Let not your sorrow die,
though I am dead"' (5.1.124–40, passim).

Nasty havoc. But do his ill deeds have a point?

Certainly: Aaron tells us about the substance of the religious in
Shakespeare. He contrasts with the explicitly devout Lucius, whose
sacrifice of Alarbus began the play's chain of revenges and dismemberments. Aaron signifies atheistical integrity, a 'truth-to-self' that
no one can shake. In fact, he performs the truest act of sacrifice in
the play, far more difficult and painful than any melodramatic show
that Titus puts on, because it amounts to a Judas-like giving of self
for cause. Shakespeare did not forget that Christianity tells the story
of two *other* sacrifices, two victim dramas: that of Judaism, skewered
on a new interpretive template; and of Judas, who roasted eternally
for his prop-like necessity as the Designated Faithless, the One Who

Betrays. In this sense, Aaron (whose name recalls that of the Jewish patriarch) gives himself up to the Romans, the victorious order. And, in so doing, he admits a criminality that makes victors and survivors feel better about themselves.

His is an odd form of generosity – a sacrificial confession, an out-of-bounds account of his deeds designed to provoke rage and exonerate the Andronici:

> I play'd the cheater for thy father's hand,
> And when I had it, drew myself apart,
> And almost broke my heart with extreme laughter.
> I pried me through the crevice of a wall,
> When, for his hand, he had his two sons' heads,
> Beheld his tears, and laugh'd so heartily
> That both mine eyes were rainy like to his . . .

> (5.1.111–17)

'Irreligious' Aaron's suicidal gesture here is blessedly self-abnegating, for by inciting Lucius's rage and directing violence towards himself, he attempts to allow his child to survive him. (By way of contrast: Titus, having sacrificed 22 sons to the Goth wars, thinks nothing of slaughtering another one of them if the poor dolt gets in his way, as Mutius does in Act 1.) Aaron's remarkable speech does something else too: it reveals the complex pleasure of violence and revenge. Unlovely, to be sure, but it grants him access outside the pale of the play he is in, to tell us of the play he writes.

He is not only the central plotter of the drama; he is the genre theorist, who understands precisely the emotional effect of a play such as *Titus Andronicus*. Aaron knows that laughter makes us complicit in violence. While this aphorism sounds more puritanical than I'd like, it describes an operation central to the horror of the play: the conflation of fairytale chills with slapstick dismemberments and ghastly assaults. The play makes us so uncomfortable because so much of the violence – unwatchable, unthinkable – is also undeniably absurd and thus amusing. Specifically, Aaron explains his deeds as an attempt to extract an emotional reaction – hoping arson victims will quench the fires with their tears, sustaining sorrow by digging up bodies – but something else, as well. He reveals his response to the play he writes, the torments he inflicts, as a paradoxical *identification* with his victim: his own laughter over Titus's plight almost breaks his heart (note that 'drew myself apart' sounds like a Titus-esque auto-dismemberment). That response recalls Titus's own inappropriate laughter in the midst of grief (3.1.264). And when he spies Titus's most ignoble duping, he laughs until he cries, 'That both mine eyes were rainy like to his.'

It is pure mockery and taunt. But Aaron's speech also sharply and strangely reflects on a critical failing of the Andronici: their inability to imagine the experience of others. This coldness, too evident in the slaughter of Alarbus against his mother's desperate pleas, extends to their own family. When Lavinia is hideously dismembered and raped, the Andronici spend a lot of time lamenting their own misery, flaunting their sad and tearful transformation, and in Marcus's case, sickeningly projecting onto her their erotic desires. Appalling. Aaron throws into relief the dull psyches and crippled ethics of Lucius and his father, who cannot empathize, who cannot enjoy or recognize the moral status of their own violence, who pretend to sacred motives in the play of power, and whose own luxurious lolling in misery deprives them of the martyrdom they seek.

Lucius reveals much about himself when he pronounces punishment on Aaron:

LUCIUS.   Set him breast-deep in earth, and famish him,
           There let him stand and rave and cry for food.
           If any one relieves or pities him,
           For the offense he dies. This is our doom.
           Some stay to see him fast'ned in the earth.

                                                   (5.3.179–83)

It is not enough to order him starved to death, a pointed-enough torment in this orally obsessed drama. Lucius must also imagine Aaron as a squalling starving baby, 'set breast-deep' in mother earth. Lucius resents Aaron's claim to generativity and nurturance, his commitment to his child. Lucius compellingly wishes to create out of his villainous other a figure of abortive birth, half-out of the womb and stuck, unnourished. But such a figure better describes the Andronici, who are between genders, wallowing in their infantile tears while they try to appropriate the care and sentiment they have in other respects destroyed.

Aaron at last wishes he were 'a devil, | To live and burn in everlasting fire, | So I might have your company in hell, | But to torment you with my bitter tongue!' (5.1.147–50). But it seems unlikely that Shakespeare would consign him there. Aaron's clarity is too great, his stance outside the ideological and dramatic frame he observes is too coherent and important to make such eternal verbal torment worth his while. His role in the play is partly to inject comic insouciance – 'Villain, I have done thy mother' (4.2.76) – and thus lighten the mood of the Andronici's deadly self-regard. But, more importantly, Aaron stands for sacrifice: by offering a Marlovian confession of villainy so humorously sharp and excessive, he allows the warring, ethically compromised Romans a great sigh of moral relief. He redeems them.

The monastery is in ruins, but devilish Aaron is discovered hiding there. And a good thing, too: for without his marvelous last line – 'If one good deed in all my life I did | I do repent it from my very soul' (5.3.189–90) – we would not have the proper perspective on what counts as a true act of repentance. Aaron *performs* the good by claiming he repents it. He scapegoats himself, exaggerates moral polarities. When he says he has 'done a thousand dreadful things, | As willingly as one would kill a fly' (5.1.141–2), we recall that Titus, in an earlier (possibly non-Shakespearean) scene, lamented much over a fly his brother killed – until his brother remarks that the fly, black, looks like Aaron. At which point crazy Titus attacks the dead bug.

*   *   *   *   *   *   *   *

I have spent perhaps a disproportionate amount of time with this play. That is because *Titus Andronicus* fires the opening salvo in Shakespeare's long godless career: the drama parodies ceremonies intended to honor the divine presence, or mocks divinity's efficacy and probability (see, for instance, the lame arrows Titus and his family shoot heavenward). Time after time in Shakespeare, subscribers to religion abuse their position, mistake their warrant and their God's intent, deform spiritual language or teachings – 'Receive the blood' (5.2.197) – erase the founding documents with a self-interested piety that amounts to incoherence. Frequently, as with Aaron, villainy sustains or propounds models of truth or virtue that 'virtue' itself cannot hope to match. Like Aaron, another cultural outsider, Shylock, exhibits a surprising rectitude that shows the dominant, the 'good,' to be something less than that. Shylock sets the Venetian Christians' profitable thievery in bright outline when he says of his own frugal prudence: 'And thrift is blessing, if men steal it not' (1.3.90). This creed proleptically interprets a good portion of the play. Godlessness (or, in Shylock's case, counter-belief) passes the ethics test in Shakespeare that Christianity, religiosity, and self-conscious virtue so often and so glaringly flunk.

Aaron, for one, apprehends and ironically embodies the underlying energy of the Christian story. He appreciates the generic shift from the tragic fact of sacrifice to the comic experience of that fact. Although he frames it as villainy, he also has a perfect grasp of what it means to offer himself for the sake of others, even to the extent of making them forget their own depredations. For that alone, he deserves the thanks of the wretched victors, the undeserving, the fly-killers.

12 The Life to Come

Macbeth

The funniest Shakespeare play? *Macbeth*.

This claim might trouble those who take the genre of tragedy seriously, and those who see the play as a test case for Shakespeare's engagement with the supernatural and the religious. It is important to distinguish between these two terms, however, and in Scotland they can work at cross purposes, so to speak.

The comedy is an integral part of godlessness, or at least of issues that arise unclearly from the world beyond. Humor in the play primarily spins off of the hostile supernatural realm – the region of unlikeness, where (for the witches, at least) men are but 'swine' (1.3.2) to be killed, and where laws of nature either cannot function reliably or do so in a laughable and frightening way. In a conversation following the murder of Duncan, Lennox tells Macbeth about the bizarre evening they have passed, and his host concurs:

LENNOX.   The night has been unruly. Where we lay,
            Our chimneys were blown down, and (as they say)
            Lamentings heard i'th'air; strange screams of death
            [. . .]
                           . . . Some say, the earth
            Was feverous and did shake.

MACBETH.   'Twas a rough night.
                         (*Macbeth*, 2.3.54–61)

Can the actor playing Macbeth deliver that line without drawing a laugh from the audience, or can the reader pass it by without wondering if Macbeth is clowning, maybe testing the limits of his own powers and ability to dissemble? Framing the events as rumor ('as they say . . . Some say'), Lennox describes a phenomenon half-off the margins of his perception, but which scared him anyway; Macbeth confirms the rumors with hilarious understatement: 'That was some gullywasher.'

The joke is good enough for Shakespeare to use it again in the following scene, with a similarly reluctant report of even-worse-boding events. Ross talks to an Old Man about an eclipse, apparently nature's response to Duncan's death. Note the comic timing, the 'wait for it . . .' punchline panache:

ROSS.   Ha, good father,
       Thou seest the heavens, as troubled with man's act,
       Threatens his bloody stage. By th'clock 'tis day,
       And yet dark night strangles the traveling lamp.
       [. . .]
OLD MAN.   'Tis unnatural,
       Even like the deed that's done. . . .
       [. . .]
ROSS.   And Duncan's horses (a thing most strange and certain),
       Beauteous and swift, the minions of their race,
       Turn'd wild in nature, broke their stalls, flung out,
       Contending 'gainst obedience, as they would make
       War with mankind.
OLD MAN. [*probable line reading: really long pause.*] 'Tis said they
       eat each other.
ROSS.   [*probable line reading: embarrassed reply.*] They did so
       – to th'amazement of mine eyes
       That look'd upon't.

                                       (2.4.4–19)

Shouldn't the sight of horses eating each other be the *first* thing that Ross reports, rather than the fact they escaped their stalls? Surely such a tale would blot out even an eclipse. That he is practically forced to confirm the event is quite funny; clearly, he was not going to mention this portent. The exchange has the quality of grotesque comedy, but it also distills something essential about the play: when nature breaks its stalls and contends against obedience, even when it looks like a 'war with mankind' is coming, the system paradoxically self-corrects: horses eat each other, one Mac- kills another Mac-, and people have little say in the matter.

Supernatural figures and events, in other words, signify a system out of balance, and out of human control; they generate terrors, but also comic possibilities or opportunities. And those suggest a threat to the interpretation of things.

A few further humorous signposts in the play lead us to rethink the supernatural. The appearance of Banquo's ghost at Macbeth's ill-fated banquet generates hijinks around Lady Macbeth's attempt to play the royal hostess. Since only Macbeth sees the ghost of the man he has killed, the new king's reaction to the appearance of Banquo has a riotous, laughworthy potential. Macbeth set up the comic trouble a few scenes before, when he was convincing the nameless murderers to dispatch Banquo. They agree to 'perform what you command us' (3.1.126) and are about to profess some deeper loyalty when he cuts them off with a howler: 'Your spirits shine through you' (3.1.127).[1] Sure they do. Soon, he receives word of Banquo's death from one of the killers: Fleance has escaped, but 'Banquo's safe,' the killer confirms: 'safe in a ditch he bides, | With twenty trenched gashes on his head, | The least a death to nature' (3.4.25–7). Horrible words, of course, and Macbeth replies: 'Thanks for that.' As if he'd just received the salt for his meat, but no greater favor. Distracted thus, he enters into one of his characteristic trances, and his wife notices his breach of manners: 'My royal lord, | You do not give the cheer' (3.4.31–2). But things only get worse as they get funnier. Banquo's Ghost enters *and sits in Macbeth's place* (s.d.). The new king cannot find a chair ('The table's full'), and begins to freak out: 'Which of you have done this? . . . Thou canst not say I did it'

(3.4.48–9). But the real comic payoff comes with his wife's compensatory social graces before the alarmed guests:

> Sit, worthy friends; my lord is often thus,
> And has been from his youth. Pray you keep seat.
> The fit is momentary . . .
> Feed, and regard him not. – Are you a man?

> (3.4.52–7)

Pay no attention! she says. But then, attempting to convince her
husband that he is not hallucinating, she helpfully informs him:
'When all's done, | You look but on a stool' (3.4.66–7). It's just a
damned chair!

How could Shakespeare get away with this? Lady Macbeth, to be
sure, does not realize she's being so funny; the comedy goes out to
the audience, does not stay onstage. And the tone shifts marvelously
to subtle horror and equivocation in a moment: 'Do not muse at
me, my most worthy friends,' Macbeth assures them, 'I have a
strange infirmity, which is nothing | To those that know me'
(3.4.84–6). But then the Ghost returns, and Macbeth screams
again, and Lady Macbeth unsuccessfully attempts to cover for her
unhinged husband: all in all, the scene cries out for John Cleese and
Prunella Scales in the lead roles. (Come to think of it, *Fawlty Towers*
could be a fairly effective adaptation of *Macbeth*.)

There are two ways to take this stage business. The first is that
the comedy and the horror work in synergy, each increasing the
other's effect. Such a reading tracks with the plot itself; Macbeth
discovers that the great prophecies guiding his future ultimately and
surprisingly take the form of a joke. When is a man not of woman
born? When he's of woman untimely torn! But the second under-
standing is theological: the farcical comedy *cancels out* the horror.
Giving the supernatural over to slapstick allows for a deep unseriousness about eschatology to enter and triumph over the play. This
quality cannot be equated with frivolity; rather, it has more to do

with subversion, with undermining accepted ranges of meaning. And indeed, we must pass through this comic unseriousness to reach a deeper horror.

Not every humorous moment in the play *directly* involves Macbeth or the supernatural. In the tricksy testing of motives and character that occurs between Macduff and Malcolm in Act 4, Scene 3, we are hard pressed to locate the most mirthful aspect: Is it in Malcolm's overblown (but not necessarily inaccurate) account of his own demerits and moral blemishes? Or in Macduff's almost obscene willingness to accommodate Malcolm's projected crimes, including rape and property seizure, in order to secure a stable kingship? The scene seems to lack a supernatural component until Malcolm, pushing hard at the limits of Macduff's support, argues that he himself, practically inhuman, has no good qualities at all:

MACDUFF.   . . . All these are portable,
            With other graces weighed.

MALCOLM.   But I have none. The king-becoming graces,
            As justice, verity, temp'rance, stableness . . .
            [. . .]
            I have no relish of them, but abound
            In the division of each several crime,
            Acting it many ways. Nay, had I pow'r, I should
            Pour the sweet milk of concord into hell,
            Uproar the universal peace, confound
            All unity on earth.

                                    (4.3.89–100)

Ludicrously enough, Macduff believes him, and cries out his protest at last: 'O nation miserable!' (4.3.103). But what makes this exchange remarkable – along with how long it takes Macduff to object – is Malcolm's articulation, almost a ventriloquizing, of the signature Macbeth fantasy. The two characters uncannily share a vision of apocalypse, universal destruction, and a desire to bring that about:

MACBETH.   I conjure you, by that which you profess
(Howe'er you come to know it), answer me:
Though you untie the winds and let them fight
Against the churches; though the yesty waves
Confound and swallow navigation up . . .
[. . .]
                                        . . . though the treasure
Of nature's germains [seeds] tumble all together,
Even till destruction sicken; answer me
To what I ask you.

                                                      (4.1.50–61)

Malcolm's comic pushing of boundaries culminates in and echoes Macbeth's vision of *no boundaries*, where churches are destroyed by witches, oceans overbear the shores, and all distinction is lost. This vision goes beyond conventional horror, or genre for that matter. And it does not have much humor about it.

But Shakespeare cannot hold out long, and finally delivers the most brazenly comic moment in his tragedies. Macbeth, facing certain defeat, calls for the man who turns out to be his valet:

MACBETH.   Seyton! – I am sick at heart,
When I behold – Seyton I say! – This push
Will cheer me ever, or disseat me now.
I have liv'd long enough . . .
[. . .]
Seyton!

SEYTON.   What's your gracious pleasure?

                                                      (5.3.19–30)

We have been prepared for this Seyton/Satan – the Porter already convinced us that Macbeth has turned Inverness into hell – but the dramaturgy here makes a joke of eschatology. Our first indication that Macbeth has a personal relationship with hell's CEO turns the play momentarily into a parody of Marlowe's *Dr. Faustus*, or a reminder of his *Edward II*, with the Luciferian murderer 'Lightborne.' This particular Seyton is urbanely sinister to the point of comedy; he enters smarmily, and he rejects Macbeth's order for armor with an amusingly laconic ''Tis not needed yet' (5.3.33). To put Seyton on stage as a disguised valet, the *diablo ex machina*, is to cause chuckles, not terrors.

And then, another oscillation: the text insinuates, from his exits and entrances, that Seyton likely kills Lady Macbeth. And his last line in the play – 'The Queen, my lord, is dead' (5.5.16) – sparks Macbeth's astonishing 'To-morrow and to-morrow' soliloquy, about which more in a moment. So clearly the comic can lead into, or produce, flat horror.

Still, Shakespeare repeatedly defuses the threat from beyond, making ghosts, portents, demonic manifestations effectively unserious; he invests the drama with a streak of buffoonery, which sorts oddly with all that is at stake. Much about the play harrows us with fear and wonder. But in taking away from the supernatural the gravitas which authorizes it, Shakespeare gives to his most cosmically subjected hero and to the audience the rationale for a new orientation toward orthodoxy.

By way of tonal contrast, the *religious* element in *Macbeth* – represented by the claim of Jacobean Divine Right which the play on one level seems to endorse – controls a serious, conflicted discourse about God's participation in the rituals and properties of kingship. Macduff's description of Duncan's murder sets out the position: 'Most sacrilegious murder hath broke ope | The Lord's anointed temple, and stole thence | The life o'th'buiding' (2.3.67–9). For those in the audience who wish to credit God's hand in monarchy, corroborating testimony comes from Malcolm's report of the English King Edward I and his sacred power to cure scrofula:

MACDUFF.   What's the disease he means?

MALCOLM.   'Tis called the evil:
               A most miraculous work in this good king,
               Which often, since my here-remain in England,
               I have seen him do. How he solicits heaven,
               Himself best knows; but strangely-visited people,
               All swoll'n and ulcerous, pitiful to the eye,
               The mere despair of surgery, he cures . . .

(4.3.146–52)

We cannot miss the fact that, syntactically, 'A most miraculous work' equals 'the evil' – blessed cures and dismal things are mirrors. The comic-supernatural and the sacred-monarchical both operate and impinge on, contaminate, each other and the world; if kingship has any purity, or partakes of the godhead, you'd never know it in Scotland or in England, despite Malcolm's attempted tribute. Take these examples of divine monarchy and its trappings in the play: Duncan's supposed blessedness but demonstrable fecklessness and venality; the mysterious disappearance of Fleance, the legendary founder of King James's line, and the absence of any prophecy about his return; the failure to account for Donalbain, the missing brother, who might have a word or two to say about Malcolm's unprotested kingship; Malcolm himself, a truly vile scrap of humanity, who seems ready to resurrect Duncan's rule, complete with potential rebellions a-brewing; Malcolm's uncanny resemblance to the allegedly evil Macbeth (including both men's tendency to fabricate words: 'here-remain', 'more-having', 'be-all and end-all'); and the facilitating Macduff, hammerheaded tool of divine right, a wife- and mother-killer who claims a righteous anger that he has not innocently earned.

The rot in kingship must pollute on the idea that any god influences the events; earthly rule this lousy should activate questions about the power and goodness, or even the presence, of divinity. Cosmic rationality comes intensely into question, and only in part because of the comic effects of supernatural weirdness. But in facing down this comedy and the misery that is kingship, Macbeth redefines the play's sense of the heroic: it comes to signify an extremity of suffering that can exceed or at least 'memorize another Golgotha' (1.2.40).

Macbeth's traffic with the supernatural gives him an extraordinary, unique celebrity: of all men who ever lived, Macbeth can be entirely certain that transhuman powers exist; and, worst of all, that they target, hoodwink, and victimize *him*. And him alone. It's a remarkable knowledge to have – in some way, precisely what he wants, the proof of his exceptionalism. And Macbeth has the nearly unimaginable courage not to be daunted by this knowledge but rather to say exactly what it means.

It means nothing.

Instead of buckling under the weight of universal forces aligned against him, instead of interpreting (as moralistic critics would have him do) his predicament as the condign response of the cosmos to the evil that he embodies etc., he transforms his comprehension to a new vision of life. Once, that life was a realm shaped to his mind, a place that accommodated itself to his fantasies, but now it has become empty, a stage and a narrative stuffed with the noisy rage of an inconclusive battle scene:

> Life's but a walking shadow, a poor player,
> That struts and frets his hour upon the stage,
> And then is heard no more. It is a tale
> Told by an idiot, full of sound and fury,
> Signifying nothing.

> (5.5.24–8)

The bravery of this philosophical conclusion is perfectly continuous with that of his earlier battlefield rampages: both are expressions of essence as Macbeth lives it. Now he frighteningly steps outside his place in historical fiction to gaze at his role as a player: one of the King's Men, Shakespeare's company, about to be

'heard no more' in this part. This self-referentiality should terrify
the audience, for he also gazes at us, at our emptiness. His role
seems in some ways opposite to his earlier identity – he *was* the
king's man who became the king, a man of purpose, loyal murder-
ing thane, royal murderer – for now it reveals itself as a purely
existential position. But instead of lamenting the battle as meaningless, or the role as empty, he embraces the final act that he can
perform, simply because he can perform it: 'Yet I will try the last'
(5.8.32). He becomes the early modern drama's finest existentialist,
taking meaning from his act.

*   *   *   *   *   *   *   *

When in the Renaissance an actor knew his lines by heart, he was
said to be 'perfect' in them; when a soldier was trained to a reliable
routine, he too was 'perfect' in his exercises. These two meanings
converge when Macbeth expresses his deepest fantasy, one that takes
him beyond acting or soldiery. Ironically, he first voices this wish
when he finds that safety eludes him:

> Then comes my fit again. I had else been perfect,
> Whole as the marble, founded as the rock,
> As broad and general as the casing air;
> But now I am cabin'd, cribb'd, confin'd, bound in
> To saucy doubts and fears –

> (3.4.20–4)

In the condition he imagines – imperviousness, permanence,
ubiquity – he strangely emulates only lifeless objects (marble, rock,
air). His notion of perfection depends on death, Banquo's death. He
used his focal word once before, telling the murderers he wears his
health 'but sickly in [Banquo's] life, | Which in his death were per-
fect' (3.1.106–7).

Here is the desire he is punished for: the desire to be perfect.
Perhaps at some level, too, this is a deeply religious desire: 'But I say

unto you, love your enemies. . . . You shall therefore be perfect, as your Father which is in heaven is perfect' (Matthew 5.48). Shakespeare activates a single, astonishing clue to suggest that Macbeth may be right to think this within reach:

THIRD WITCH.   All hail, Macbeth, that shalt be King hereafter!
BANQUO.   Good sir, why do you start, and seem to fear
                Things that do sound so fair?

                                        (1.3.50–2)

The frightening thing is not 'King;' it is 'hereafter.' Banquo's question shows us the effect of the idea on his friend. 'Hereafter' could mean 'later, eventually;' but it does not. The word at this moment in the play takes on the force of 'forever.' All hail Macbeth, king of eternity! The idea of his reigning 'hereafter' explains the pernicious effect of the prophecies, the contradictions of which Macbeth deliberately fails to interpret; their meanings would be transparent to one who did not already half-believe in his own invulnerability. We are far now from the humor that animates much of the supernatural in the story, and far too from the religious perspective that poisons an insight into kingship. By the end of the story, the shattering oppressive word clarifies his otherwise baffling response to his wife's death: 'She should have died hereafter.' Catch the bitterness of that pronouncement, the self-mockery of his mortal recognition. He does not mean she should or would have died 'later' or 'eventually;' he means that she, like he, ought to have received what they were virtually promised: never to have died. Then, to be sure, 'There would have been a time for such a word' (5.5.18).

His urge for perfection pitches him towards the godhead absent from the play, an absence that Macbeth, and no one else, apprehends and approaches. For that urge and his final station of existential clarity he must be rewarded, at least in our minds: his single, crucial interpretation is his licensed imagination of forever, the idea that he could, in the right circumstances, 'jump the life to come' (1.7.7). In Macbeth's mind, he can leap beyond even the afterlife. He cannot know where that will put him. But unlike the palterers left behind, it's a risk he is more than willing to take.

13 Dreams of Sex and Death

Bottom

Coming to himself in the dark wood, abandoned by his frightened friends after his transformation, Bottom in *A Midsummer Night's Dream* arrives at a fine thought: 'but I will not stir from this place, do what they can. I will walk up and down here, and I will sing, that they shall hear I am not afraid' (3.1.121–4).

He *is* afraid because he is alone, but soon he is neither. His singing wakes Titania with a beauty only she can grasp. And grasp she does, vise-clamping the lost weaver as if he were her found child. Which of course he is – beloved substitute for the 'little changeling boy' (2.1.120) whom Titania refused to give to Oberon.

Disturbingly, by the terms of the spell, Titania is supposed to 'wake when some vile thing is near' (2.2.34). But the fact that she wakes in proximity to the gentle and inoffensive Bottom signifies only the fallibility and confusion of the fairy world, its tendency to produce mistaken magical disorder it must then scramble to correct.

Bottom's ensuing interlude with Titania, commingling wish and worry, sex and spirit, gives him a range of things he has long dreamed of: social mobility, beloved centrality, potency. And also some things his desire may not have reckoned: a high-status role as queen's consort and king-substitute (Titania orders a crown of flowers for him); a phase of second childhood via sexual bondage; and a trip to the edge of promised immortality.

Viewers who see Nick Bottom as the recipient of a miracle can be excused for trying to feed data about him through the Christian calculator. Certainly, Bottom's demeanor as the oblivious innocent, to whom something amazing happens, invites a Gospel-tinged intervention. He may be susceptible to his magical encounter because he has some of the characteristics of an unvarnished believer: he lacks guile, cynicism, doubt. Almost completely incapable of surprise, at least until he awakes, Bottom remembers the childlike ability to know his experience sweetly, without complication, without remorse.

But he's neither holy nor touched by the divine. Once he slides into magical asshood he sees neither God, nor the kingdom of heaven, although he stumbles around the verbal trappings of these myths. He finds instead a dream that, like the forest-dreams of every other major character in the play, fulfills embarrassing, compelling urges, most of them explicitly social or erotic. The once-feckless blusterer of the play swims in an inexpressible access of wish-fulfillment, and he grows complete in his pragmatic acceptance of the place that God does not have in his life.

*   *   *   *   *   *   *

In his translated state, Bottom acknowledges Titania's love, absorbs her sexual threats – 'Thou shalt remain here, whether thou wilt or no' (3.2.153) – receives promises of flower beds and immortality, and then meets her mini-courtiers: Peaseblossom, Cobweb, Moth; and one last fellow, Mustardseed, who exhibits a quality Bottom finds bracing: 'Good Master Mustardseed, I know your patience well. That same cowardly, giant-like ox-beef hath devour'd many a gentleman of your house: I promise you your kindred hath made my eyes water ere now' (3.1.191–5). What seems to be teary sympathy for the plight of the devoured mustardseed clan is just bodily reaction to spicy vapors – a witty joke that Bottom probably would have been incapable of just a few minutes before. Despite his watery eyes, he would 'desire you of more acquaintance, good Master Mustardseed' (195–6).

Since Bottom gives a dollop more attention to the little guy than to his friends, let us think about why. In the Gospels, Jesus, always eager to find analogies for what he's up to, settles at one point on the lowly and miniature mustard seed to encapsulate an image of belief and salvation. He introduces the figure thus: 'And he said: whereunto shall we liken the kingdom of God? or with what comparison shall we compare it? It is like a grain of mustardseed, which, when it is sown in the earth, is less than all seeds that be in the earth: but after that it is sown, it groweth up, and is greatest of all herbs: and beareth great branches' (Mark 4.30–2).

The mustardseed story is just a simile, not a full-grown narrative parable. The bare similitude presents no interpretive hurdle; it is open, clear, and we can track its logic. That alone makes it nearly unique in Mark, the Gospel most involved in the thematics of secrecy and recondite knowledge, where Jesus stubbornly cleaves to his uninterpretability (see 4.10–13).

When Bottom says he desires Mustardseed's greater acquaintance, he seems to speak code (though he does not know it) for a salvational desire, and a conviction that patience will help him get to heaven. But the referentiality of the Mustardseed episode is beyond Bottom's conscious grasp, the words of heavenly analogy shimmering at the edges of his memory when he meets his new servant. The play of meaning functions only as an echo, accent – a grace note.

One problem with positing that the invisible sprite realm represents the heavenly sphere arises from the fairies' characteristic behavior – their strained marriages and mimetic court, their concern with the household, their stupid flighty tricks. Oberon and Titania inhabit a *horizontal* ecosystem, reflectively parallel and not superior to our own. Relatedly, Bottom's liaison with Titania (as far as we can guess) seems at least as richly physical and social – based on body, money, class – as it does religious. Something more, too: it is theatrical. For the culminating triumph of the transformation allows his surehanded return to the stage. Bottom functions as a holy fool along the Shakespearean gradient of the sacred: not like those abused Antonios, a fool for love, nor especially a 'fool for Christ's sake' who knows what he does, suffering ridicule and persecution for a higher cause of soul; but an actor of utter ingenuousness, *unconsciously* responsible for a redemption centered on art.

* * * * * * * *

After the spell has ended, Bottom arises right on cue, to the word 'dreams' (4.1.199) – and like the stellar metadramatic figure he is, his first waking line comments on his 'cue' and how he'll answer when it arrives, which it just did. Here is the weaver hitting his mark, recalling his dream:

> When my cue comes, call me, and I will answer. My next is, 'Most fair Pyramus.' Heigh-ho! Peter Quince! Flute, the bellows-mender! Snout, the tinker! Starveling! God's my life, stolen hence, and left me asleep!

> (4.1.200–4)

Bottom's 'God's my life' means, according to the *Oxford English Dictionary*, 'Good lord!'.[1] But the words signify more than a common expression of surprise; they speak a debt to divinity. And this debt evaporates immediately: Bottom records absence, not presence. For precisely as he entered his dream, so he leaves it – alone, abandoned: 'Stolen hence, and left me asleep!' The apparent referent is to his friends ('Peter Quince! . . . Starveling!'), yet Bottom's words compellingly summon the *deus absconditus* tradition, the God who has stolen hence: a God hidden from the believer. Shakespeare here recalls passages such as Isaiah 45.15 ('Truly you are a God who hides yourself, | O God of Israel, the Savior'), that painful conjunction of professed faith and depressed longing. Having been left asleep, perplexed and exposed, Bottom rises to solitude. He reorients himself in an emptied world, usefully abandoned by God.

But, then, God seems not to be required for Bottom's transcendence. Just having the right dream will do.

At the end of a life, or a life-altering interlude, some people look back, look around, and assess what has happened. If they have lived well, done little harm, been happy, they may wish to share their blessing. They may wish to tell others about their life, to suggest ways to live, to carry on. Bottom vows not to do that:

> I have had a most rare vision. I have had a dream, past the wit of man to say what dream it was. Man is but an ass if he go about t' expound this dream.

> (4.1.204–7)

Bottom thinks explication impossible. His comic 'Man is but an ass if . . .' suggests that he has left his transformation behind – renounced his assification – even as he dimly remembers it. And this renunciation amounts to a willingness to let things settle unexplained, which magically signals a truer transformation than any theater prop, any ass-head, conveys. Because earlier, his keynote was his *literalism* and his desire for over-explanation:

> There are things in this comedy of Pyramus and Thisby that will never please. [. . .] I have a device to make all well. Write me a prologue, and let the prologue seem to say we will do no harm with our swords, and that Pyramus is not kill'd indeed; and for the more better assurance, tell them that I Pyramus am not Pyramus, but Bottom the weaver. This will put them out of fear.

> (3.1.9–22)

The connection between his literalism and *fear* – his audience's and particularly his own – says a lot about the metamorphosis. The need to pronounce, identify, and delimit reveals anxiety about transgression. It pins the speaker in an identifiable place constructed for him, leaves him helpless to do anything other than over-explain, and displays his powerlessness. But after his transformation, Bottom's sense of things wanders blithely away from anxious need, from meaning tethered to frightened obligation. When critics discuss the spiritual potential of the weaver, this is their Bottom line:

> Methought I was – there is no man can tell what. Methought I was – and methought I had – but man is but a patch'd fool if he will offer to say what methought I had. The eye of man hath not heard, the ear of man hath not seen, man's hand is not able to taste, his tongue to conceive, nor his heart to report, what my dream was.
>
> (4.1.207–14)

He happily *cannot* speak the truth of what happened to him, and his not-speaking lodges him firmly in the godless world. For in tangling up Paul's language to the Corinthians, Bottom perfectly negates the Pauline message. Specifically, the apostle trumpets the verbiage of believers who are touched by the Spirit:

> But we speake the wisdome of God in a mysterie, euen the hid wisdome, which God had determined before the worlde, vnto our glorie. . . . But as it is written, The things which the eye hathe not sene, nether eare hathe heard, nether came into mans heart, are, which God hathe prepared for them that loue him. But God hathe reveiled them vnto vs by his Spirit: for the Spirit searcheth all things, yea, the deepe things of God.
>
> (Geneva Bible 1560, 1 Cor. 2.7–10)[2]

'The deepe things:' in Tyndale's 1534 rendering, we can go deeper: 'For the spirit searcheth all things, yea the bottom of God's secrets.'[3]

But if Bottom is privy to God's secrets, he cannot speak them. They remain 'in a mysterie,' 'hid wisdome' that defeats his power to explain. Bottom's memorial deconstruction of Paul not only refuses to consider future glories 'which God hathe prepared for them that loue him;' but the weaver also radically excises God and belief from his otherwise referential moment.

As Bottom discovered on first awakening, he is alone, theatrically and eschatologically. In marked contrast to his immediate fears after his transformation, however, his new solitude, post-dream, has grown to comfort and security. Something marvelous has indeed occurred. In edging towards disclosure, Bottom moves from desire to triumphant inability – from the wish to speak, to an unembarrassed muteness.

At the last, Bottom knows something beautiful and moving has happened to him, something he feels compelled to share, but he knows neither what it was nor how exactly to convey it: in the play, the ballad he plans to commission and sing of his dream also goes unsung. Tempting as it is to call his a religious experience – Paul and Mustardseed lure us there – Bottom's dream *forecloses* religion, in that it checks the aggressive certainty of the proselyte. His inenarrable rapture fuses his limited, nominal identity – 'It shall be call'd Bottom's Dream' – and the limitless possibility that negates him – 'because it hath no bottom' (4.1.215–16). And that very duality, the dream's simultaneous boundlessness and limit, causes the glossolalia of Bottom's Pauline parody. But his language trouble also comes from the decidedly non-transcendent urges of his erotic partner. For Bottom's dream began as Bottom's rape. When Titania says 'Tie up my lover's tongue, bring him silently' (3.1.201), she delivers, though we could not guess it at the time, an injunction with a lasting effect. After he awakes, still tongue-tied, he cannot tell his own story, let alone sing it.

*   *   *   *   *   *   *   *

It is my hope, as it is my belief, that death is the end. Life is pleasant and I have enjoyed it, but I have no yearning to clutter up the Universe, a shape without a habitation or a name, after it is over.
H. L. Menken[4]

A dream is an idiolect, a psychic snowflake. Though we sometimes say that art is a shared space of dream, Bottom's evocative inarticulateness tells us something else: that dreams are as individual and unique as deaths. (*The Tempest, in toto*, tells us this too.) Bottom's encounter with Titania began with the language of transcendence, as she promised to purge his 'mortal grossness so, | That thou shalt like an aery spirit go' (3.1.160–1) – in other words, to make him fleshless, immaterial, immortal. That did not happen. Which is all for the good: such an event would have meant death, the end of his earthly life. Instead, when he awakes, Bottom is born back into his mortality, and he finds it wonderful. His impulse to share his vision through song – 'I will get Peter Quince to write a ballet of this dream' (4.1.214–15) – is compellingly *social*, an attempt to re-establish community, to improve the play. The point and purpose of Bottom and his friends in *Midsummer*, as readers have noted, is to mend: to knit up rifts, to fix the tear in the social and generic fabric.

I mentioned that the primary effect of Bottom's intimation of immortality, or the possibility of having his mortal grossness purged, is to become fearless. His fretful literalism early on, shared by his fellows – 'That would hang us, every mother's son' (1.2.78) – turns at last into a strength, a brash earnestness shown when he quickly corrects his betters:

THESEUS.   The wall methinks, being sensible, should curse
            again.
PYRAMUS.   No, in truth sir, he should not. 'Deceiving me' is
            Thisby's cue. She is to enter now . . . You shall see
            it will fall pat as I told you. Yonder she comes.

                                                    (5.1.182–8)

He grows excellently, authoritatively impatient with the snide tyrannies of the audience. If his dream seems to have given him some sense of worth beyond his class, that sense may or may not derive from the wonder of invisible things; but his experience has the more significant aftereffect of removing the fear from his life, because he wakes alone, without God, and thrives.

Bottom's dream sparkles not because it is coated with Christian fairy dust, but because it was lovely to him – and he can take a small part of it, an intimation of otherness and his own much enhanced sense of value, back to the waking world. If his dream shines for us, that's because we have a chance to reflect on the comedy and complexity of an occasion that has 'no bottom,' an admirable ambivalence I take to mean: no foundation, but no end; no ballast, but no absolutely limiting significance either.

We see the surfaces of Bottom's dream, but we cannot know what it means to have lived or internalized it: to have been a weaver entwined in the arms of a fairy queen, the rough artisan cuckolding a powerful king, to be the bondsman, baby, finally the passionate revulsion and erotic regret – 'O, how mine eyes do loathe his visage now!' (4.1.79) – of a royal mistress. Such a dream is unique; but we, too, through dozy hope, or theater, or willful delusion, can glean something of an unspeakable otherness. When we know a love whose memory we can neither shake nor fully articulate, the most sensible response may be Bottom's: be grateful for the gift, the look behind the veil. Turn it into art if you can, and return to the day in full and pleasured awareness. Celebrate the wedding. Get on with the play!

Fortunately, the spirits of *A Midsummer Night's Dream*, and its humans too, do just that. The figure most responsible for the troubles and transformations, the plot catalyst Puck, abandons his taste for humiliation and does some good at the end. He manages this in two apparently opposite ways. First, he reminds the audience of death:

> Now the wasted brands do glow,
> Whilst the screech-owl, screeching loud,
> Puts the wretch that lies in woe
> In remembrance of a shroud.
> Now it is the time of night
> That the graves, all gaping wide,
> Every one lets forth his sprite,
> In the church-way paths to glide.

(5.1.375–82)

The images are appallingly messy in Mencken's sense of universal clutter: burnt-out firebrands living on after their death; noise, misery, shroud-thoughts, empty graves pouring forth souls out of place – zombie souls trying to find the church, no less. But after summoning this lamentable, *religious* immortalism, Puck also offers household blessings, saying of his mission: 'I am sent with broom before, | To sweep the dust behind the door' (5.1.389–90). Importantly, the nightmare visions inform the housework. For whether Puck is sweeping the dust hidden behind the door, or hiding the dust by sweeping it there, his act involves the twin urgencies of cleaning and concealment – an act dictated by the dust itself. Dust is something in plain sight, and also something that (one) hides. And although he says he will sweep it, he will not sweep away the idea of it. As his reminder about the wandering souls implies, he knows, as we do, that dust comprises our elemental condition, our materiality and mortality, beginning and end. It is often in our festive interest to hide or forget that. Yet Puck makes amends precisely by calling attention to it. This reminder of death at the end of comedy is common in Shakespeare – it has already occurred in *Pyramus and Thisby*'s burlesque tragedy – and it does, I believe, perform a kind of cleaning. It sweeps up the religious disarray of those wandering, placeless souls whose images he has conjured, and it deposits them in the dust. For Puck, cleanliness is next to godlessness.

Happy endings have an atheism about them. Finality makes a *cleaner* creed than the gaping, overflowing fictions of the afterlife. A universe thick with soul traffic, beset by the terrifying, primitive myths of eternity, is not a tidy place. Mencken's Puckish wish for the trim propriety of an end-stopped life expresses something true to the nature of comic spirit – what I take to be, in his best moments, Shakespeare's spirit. Uncluttering the stage of meaningless pieties, sweeping superstitions behind the door, godless Shakespeare sets about his gorgeous work, puts the house in order.

14 Her Becomings

Cleopatra

She stands, or more probably reclines, outside the world's system of tiers and orders, choosing self-images of her devising. Subject to history only insofar as she manifests there, here she *becomes*, the ringmaster of Shakespeare's sole belief. To the extent that Cleopatra's deeds are opaque, and her strategies and meanings run a gamut from petty to grandly unknowable, ordinary evaluative criteria do not apply. In particular, she cannot be made fully intelligible because she defeats any ordinary account of motive, even as she defeats Caesar, even as she beggars all description. Exceeding representation, she becomes it. It could hardly be any other way.

Cleopatra's most vehement, passionate, exquisite expressions of self and love are always undercut by irony, or context, or her own complex dissembling. The great case in point: her mindbending manipulation of Dolabella in the last act of *Antony and Cleopatra*, in which Shakespeare proves that even the most transcendent poetry and exalted love language can be put to practical use – here, scooping some data out of a reluctant observer, a man who was supposed to betray her, but ended up betraying Caesar instead. Cleopatra, that is, makes converts to her religion, and she does so through the perception of her love, described as a natural force, a gravitational pull. After hearing her reverie-like tribute to Antony, Dolabella says 'Hear me, good madam; | Your loss is as yourself, great; and you bear it | As answering to the weight' (5.2.100–2). She thanks him for his sympathy, but does not wait a beat before asking: 'Know you what

Caesar means to do with me?' (5.2.106). Even if we look back at the
lines she delivers about Antony that work this marvel – 'His delights
| Were dolphin-like, they show'd his back above | The element they
liv'd in' (5.2.88–90) – retrospectively illuminating them with our
knowledge of her motives, the words still shimmer with poetic truth,
or something like it.

When, in Act 2 of the play, Caesar's and Antony's men bond with
each other, ridiculing Lepidus and generally forecasting the dissolu-
tion of the triumvirate, they also anticipate something important
about the play's view of the historical giants that occupy the tale.
Enobarbus mentions Lepidus's great love for Caesar; Agrippa notices
how much Lepidus 'adores Mark Antony!'; Enobarbus responds that
Caesar is 'the Jupiter of men,' and concludes 'Would you praise
Caesar, say "Caesar," go no further' (3.2.7–13). The hyperbole that
feeds the leaders is parodic and absurd. And while this powerful
demythologizing exchange ridicules the play's own habit of constructing historical persons as if they were incomparable, like most
mockery, accuracy invigorates it. Enobarbus's own mode of parody
has its basis in an earlier discussion that, too, may seem empty and
jokey, but in fact has crucial meaning folded within.

The triumvirs are aboard Pompey's galley, sloshed and inquisi-
tive. Lepidus wants to learn some natural history of four-footed
beasts in Egypt, and he asks Antony: 'what manner o' thing is your
crocodile?' Antony replies:

> It is shap'd, sir, like itself, and it is as broad as it hath breadth. It
> is just so high as it is, and moves with it own organs. It lives by
> that which nourisheth it, and the elements once out of it, it trans-
> migrates.

> (2.7.41–5)

Only the last part of that description is non-redundant, or informa-
tional. And Antony concludes the report with further circularity:

LEPIDUS.　　What color is it of?
ANTONY.　　Of it own color too.

LEPIDUS.   'Tis a strange serpent.
ANTONY.   'Tis so, and the tears of it are wet.

(2.7.46–9)

It would not be that hard to provide a description of the crocodile
that would have some greater specificity than this, some photo-
graphic accuracy. We might think that Antony's just having Lepidus
on, demonstrating his superior power, humiliating him in front of
Caesar. Antony, for whatever reason, does not offer an immediately
helpful account of the crocodile. But that is not his goal.

Instead, he provides an unimprovable description of Cleopatra.

Antony's apparent non-answer to Lepidus's query moves from
silliness to centrality once the referents 'Cleopatra' and 'crocodile'
overlap. Cleopatra, if she is this strange serpent (and indeed, she's
told us that Antony calls her 'my serpent of old Nile' (1.5.25), so
the identification seems likely), becomes the inexchangable, the
indescribable. These attributes might at first suit any intensely
beloved person or object. The answer to Lepidus's question 'What
manner of thing?' can translate to a single word: 'incomparable.'
Beyond metaphor.

To defeat metaphor, to be precisely the thing she is until the elements are out of her and she transmigrates into the thing she is not,
is to transcend poetic language and analogical thought: she becomes
the ideal object of worship, inimical to poetry. Cleopatra has always
been uncertainty, indeterminacy itself. She does have episodes of
expert imitation: 'no more but e'en a woman, and commanded | By
such poor passion as the maid that milks' (4.15.73–4); the jealous
lover; the haughty imperatrix; the grand, vexing paramour. And she
has been constituted by what men say about her, derisive or abjectly
admiring, such as Enobarbus's famous description: 'Age cannot
wither her, nor custom stale | Her infinite variety' (2.2.234–5). These
attributes together, bound and pleated, ordered and color-coded, still
do not compose a plausible entity with psychic coherence. But that
tracks with her purpose.

Her purpose? Shakespeare is playing with God in the canon.

What distinguishes Cleopatra from any figure in the works, what makes her incomparable as Antony suggests, is the potent sense that her miracles of self-preservation and self-presentation are at once fully functional in history and gratuitously luminous. Not merely an empress, she is an avatar of divine play. Her much-rumoured appearance to Antony on the river Cydnus, for instance, sets the paradigm: Agrippa and Maecenus have both heard of the event, but only Enobarbus, ambivalent disciple, can 'tell you' correctly: and he shows not what a transcendent marvel she is, but how she 'O'er-pictur[es] that Venus where we see | The fancy outwork Nature' (2.2.200–1). The description continues, a wonder of paradox, and culminates with this:

ENOBARBUS.   For vilest things
          Become themselves in her, that the holy priests
          Bless her when she is riggish.

                                                        (2.2.237–9)

'Riggish': horny, concupiscent. The more interesting point, though, lies in Enobarbus's layered claim that the 'vilest things | become themselves in her:'

- they are made most beautiful, or becoming;
- they are made most perfectly themselves, most vile;
- in becoming most vile, in achieving the perfection of their quiddity, they become most beautiful;
- she becomes the container for all that is vile, and for all that is self-fulfillingly itself;
- her qualities of assumption, containment, perfection, and manifestation in her throes of sexual excess cause holy priests to bless her;
- and they are not wrong to do so.

This may be Shakespeare's most engaged account of the godly, the sacred, the imaginatively compelling.

Marvelously enough, he may be drawing from a Kabbalah tradition as much as an Egyptian one. In describing the universal
nothingness of divine creativity called Ayin, the Jewish mystical
book says that 'No one can know anything about it – except the
belief that it exists. Its existence cannot be grasped by anyone other
than it. Therefore its name is "I am becoming."'[1]

Cleopatra's 'becomings' also have more pedestrian manifestations. In a peerless bit of puppet-string-snapping, she claims (after
having needled Antony to anger) that 'my becomings kill me when
they do not | Eye well to you' (1.3.96–7). By 'becomings' she means
her virtues, and her transformations, and this context seems more
limited than meanings she later takes on. But even here, the 'Eye
well to you' aurally shifts into 'I well to you,' which suggests that
her becomings kill her if they do not translate self to other – my
becomings kill me if they do not become you. In some sense, her
transformations are contingent on a mutuality of perception and
response. And it is exactly these becomings that make her incomparable and dangerous, for they are psychic metamorphoses that do
not signify *her* transformations alone, but her transformative power
over others. The wrangling queen 'whom everything becomes'
(1.1.49) is also the nemesis that Caesar implies in his gloss on
Antony's decline: 'Observe how Antony becomes his flaw'
(3.12.34).

The play may be, as Janet Adelman established,[2] a perfect example of skepticism as a precondition of belief. 'Think you there was
or might be such a man | As this I dreamt of?' Cleopatra asks her
mesmerized listener, Dolabella. He replies: 'Gentle madam, no'
(5.2.94). The 'no' opens the gate for Dolabella to betray Caesar, giving him the integrity he needs to violate his loyalty, even as
Cleopatra's equally striking 'O, my oblivion is a very Antony, | And
I am all forgotten' entices her sweetheart's graceful demurral: 'But
that your royalty | Holds idleness your subject, I should take you |
For idleness itself' (1.3.90–3), a 'no' that nonetheless brings him
back to her – the no that means yes.

But to suggest that skepticism or denial produces belief does not, I should say, mean that belief remains secure or fixed. For a godless Shakespeare, it could not. Cleopatra makes an unstable and unreliable icon, even an icon of constant change. Belief in her resembles belief in the loving tides; it is possible, but miscalculation or negligence can kill you. Because, let's face it, she transmigrates, and the believer in such a figure finds that the divine evades him; he becomes, as most Shakespearean believers do, seeker after an absent god.

It approaches perfection that Antony's description of Cleopatra as the crocodile, a beast which cannot be metaphorized, is itself an implicit metaphor. Containing and enacting its contradictions, Antony's figure gives us a paradox of being: Cleopatra, unnamed in the comparison, bodies forth the mystery of her absence as her most precisely beautiful feature. That her absence is a referent (she is neither A nor B term, although 'Cleopatra is like a crocodile' is inescapably implied) ratifies even as it undercuts her validity. 'Your crocodile' yields no information about itself, seems self-cancellingly redundant, and if we didn't know that it transmigrates, we'd know nothing. Her missing name signifies her, even in a moment that might otherwise make her ridiculous. And her crocodile tears – the sign of the insincere monster – are never far from her becomings.

Astonishingly, though, worship happens, and it happens in the audience, the congregation. Nowhere else in Shakespeare does a character so successfully enshrine herself as a legitimate object of devotion:

> Give me my robe, put on my crown, I have
> Immortal longings in me.

(5.2.280–1)

The asp-bringing clown has just told us that the bite of the 'worm' is 'immortal,' for 'those that do die of it do seldom or never recover' (5.2.247–8). Truer than he knows: Cleopatra, in the most spectacular of her self-aggrandizing formations, moves toward that state of imaginative energy that any God or holy manifestation requires. The clown, his speech guiding us into this palace of worship, talks of a woman who died of the worm, who 'makes a very good report o'th'worm; but he that will believe all that they say, shall never be sav'd by half that they do' (5.2.255–7). Cleopatra, crocodile and dedicated narcissist, has become now the serpent worm, consummating her own immortal longings. When Caesar, who was tricked into believing all she said, enters after her death, he does not begrudge her her magic; he even manages a 'becoming' himself, a transformation, by describing her devoutly:

> She looks like sleep,
> As she would catch another Antony
> In her strong toil of grace.

(5.2.346–8)

'Toil' is a net, and, sometimes, grace does not descend unbidden; sometimes, you have to snare it, be snared by it. Cleopatra's toil also suggests grace as a *work*, her final religious/spiritual production, for her greatest art reveals her determinedly hard at play, with the effects irresistible anyway. She becomes a founding exemplum for a religion that merges faith and works. But that religion's believers have all perished, like the flawlessly spoken phonemes of a lost language that cannot use metaphor.

As in the sacrifice of the productions of the earth in cult, the production of the *holy* effects a rotation of the significance of words toward the origin of significance in God, who is outside of experience and therefore outside language. As he is aniconic – without image because perfectly free – so also he is antimetaphoric – a 'man of war' who defeats comparison. 'Who is like you, majestic in holiness?' (Ex. 15.11).[3]

When the weight that Cleopatra bears lessens and lifts, when her death approaches, what becomes of her? She tells us herself: she transforms into fire and air, male elements to be sure, but weightless ones; and she leaves the massy earth of flesh and fluids where she has played. Her magnificent passing has not a trace of sorrow about it, and, though it is deeply ambivalent, it is also a wild success. She manages to escape imminent captivity and humiliation; to nurse the serpentine baby, Death; to spin the orgasmic fiction of reuniting with Antony as his husband ('Husband, I come'); to stage a pansexual performance of trans-erotics with herself and her beloved girls, sirs, servants. The question must be not how to interpret this crowning moment, but how the moment itself interprets, or produces meaning, of everything around it. And here we see her godliness – her beyond-godliness. The ruler of the propertied world enters and utters a truly lovely, subtle tribute; in performance, the glistering language ('She looks like sleep . . .') ought to surprise even him. If she can transform Caesar into a poet, she can do anything.

*   *   *   *   *   *   *

The part Caesar plays – ambitious toady of death, the 'universal landlord' who wishes to cover Cleopatra with his 'shroud' (3.3.71–2) – includes a turn as the unknowing usher and valet of the New Religion. Historically, the cliché has it that global peace, the pax Romana, had to reign in order for Christ's peace to come into the world. And the calculus could not be clearer: for Christ to be born, for peace to prevail, Cleopatra and Antony have to die. Perhaps this exchange seems to some in Shakespeare's culture a plus.

Cleopatra anticipates (or, from the Renaissance era's perspective, reiterates) a central tenet of that new faith: 'My desolation does begin to make | A better life' (5.2.1–2). Yet this life, afterlife, belongs only to her: radically unlike her Christ antitype, she has no interest at all in making of her losses a better life for anyone else. And though, like other deities, she prepares for her own transmigration, moving from 'no more but e'en a woman' to 'nothing | Of woman in me' (5.2.238–9), she gives us nothing to believe in, while gracefully bestowing amazement.

For Cleopatra is not only a performer; she is a *performance*. In this she embodies the elements of religion implicit in Shakespearean practice: theatrical, dependent on the material and maternal presence, an intricate cathedral-carnival of prayer and play. But as with her crown, which Charmian notes at Cleopatra's death is 'awry,' her image requires, at the last, mending. Even a god who can be anything needs maintenance.

Thus Cleopatra the crocodile finally becomes something intangible: Desire. So perverse, transformative, slithery, and always just out of reach. She is unquestionably Shakespeare's God.

Shakespeare has an idea about a deity worthy of worship. But it has to be the God *he* makes.

Notes

Quotations and line numbers from Shakespeare's text are from *The Riverside Shakespeare*, ed. G. Blakemore Evans *et al.* (Boston: Houghton Mifflin Co., 1997).

Introduction

1. Conversation with Stephen Greenblatt, October 2005, Austin, Texas.
2. Lucien Febvre, *The Problem of Unbelief in the Sixteenth Century: The Religion of Rabelais*, trans. Beatrice Gottlieb (Cambridge, MA: Harvard University Press, 1982).
3. See Robert Hunter, *Shakespeare and the Mystery of God's Judgments* (Athens, Georgia: University of Georgia Press, 1979).
4. Joseph Ritson, *Remarks, critical and illustrative, on the text and notes of the last edition of Shakespeare* (London, 1783), p. 188. Quoted in Gary Sloan, 'Was Shakespeare an Atheist?', *American Atheist* 38, no. 4 (2000): 22.
5. George Santayana, 'The Absence of Religion in Shakespeare,' in *Interpretations of Poetry and Religion* (New York: Harper and Bros., 1957), pp. 147–65; 152.
6. Carlo Ginzburg, *The Cheese and the Worms: The Cosmos of a Sixteenth Century Miller*, trans. John and Anne Tedeschi (Baltimore, MD: Johns Hopkins University Press, 1980).
7. David Wootton and Michael Hunter, eds, *Atheism from the Reformation to the Enlightenment* (Oxford: Oxford University Press, 1992); Richard H. Popkin, (see Further Reading); Alan C. Kors, *Atheism in France, 1650–1729* (Princeton: Princeton University Press,

1990); Jennifer M. Hecht, *Doubt: A History* (San Francisco: Harper San Francisco, 2003); David Riggs and Robert N. Watson, (see Further Reading).

8. Jonathan Dollimore, 'Afterword,' in Ewan Fernie, ed., *Spiritual Shakespeares* (London: Routledge, 2005), p. 214.

Chapter 1

1. For a brief account of the high-risk roll that Oppenheimer thought he was taking, see Richard Rhodes, *The Making of the Atomic Bomb* (New York: Simon and Schuster, 1986), pp. 418–9.

2. Jack Miles, *God: A Biography* (New York: Alfred A. Knopf, 1995), p. 311.

3. John Donne, 'Death's Duel,' from *Devotions Upon Emergent Occasions* (Ann Arbor, Michigan: University of Michigan Press, 1959), pp. 176–7.

4. Francis Bacon, 'Of Atheism,' in *Francis Bacon: Selected Writings*, ed. H. Dick (New York: Random House, 1955). p. 46.

5. I owe the Shakespearean application of this theology to Robert G. Hunter, *Shakespeare and the Mystery of God's Judgments* (cited above), pp. 20–38.

Chapter 3

1. 'Replacement Theology' is also commonly known as 'supersessionism'. On Irenaeus, see Elaine Pagels, *Beyond Belief* (see Further Reading), pp. 151–4.

2. Michael J. Vlach, 'Augustine's Contribution to Supersessionism,' at www.theologicalstudies.citymax.com/articles/article/1546226/17518.htm, *Theological Studies.org* (25 November 2004; accessed August 2006). See also John G. Gager, *The Origins of Anti-Semitism: Attitudes Toward Judaism in Pagan and Christian Antiquity* (New York and Oxford: Oxford University Press, 1983), pp. 155–6, pp. 162–7.

3. On 'the Jewishness of the Gospel,' see John Shelby Spong, *Liberating the Gospels: Reading the Bible with Jewish Eyes* (San Francisco: Harper

San Francisco, 1996); Alexander Tarasenko, 'Jesus and His parables in the context of Rabbinic Judaism,' *Acta patristica et byzantina* 12 (2001): 179–97. See also Anon., 'A Refutation of Replacement Theology,' at www.geocities.com/israeltour/ 20000105RepTheo.html.
4. Ignacio L. Götz, 'Surrogate Motherhood,' *Theology Today* 45 no. 2 (1988): 189–95; 192.
5. The student was M. Mullins, English 321, Fall 2005, University of Texas at Austin.

Chapter 4

1. More respectable commentators than Cartman have thought so. 'Jesus Christ – who, as it turns out, was born of a virgin, cheated death, and rose bodily into the heavens – can now be eaten in the form of a cracker. A few Latin words spoken over your favorite Burgundy, and you can drink his blood as well. Is there any doubt that a lone sub-scriber to these beliefs would be considered mad? Rather, is there any doubt that he would *be* mad?" Sam Harris, *The End of Faith* (see Further Reading), p. 73.
2. *South Park*, 'Do the Handicapped go to Hell?,' original air date 19 July 2000; Trey Parker and Matt Stone (Warner Bros.: Comedy Central Television, Season 4, disc 2, 2000).
3. John Bridges, *A Sermon preached at Paules Crosse on the Monday in Whitson weeke Anno Domini 1571* (London, 1571), p. 125.
4. I thank Matt Doloff for this reference.
5. 'Scott Tenorman Must Die,' original air date 11 July 2001; *South Park: Insults to Injuries* (Warner Bros., Comedy Central Television, 2002).
6. *The Passion of the Christ*, dir. Mel Gibson (20th Century Fox, 2004).

Chapter 5

1. The seminal treatment of Christlike characters named Antonio comes from Cynthia Lewis, '"Wise men, folly-fall'n:" Characters Named Antonio in English Renaissance Drama,' chapter 1 of her *Particular Saints: Shakespeare's Four Antonios, Their Contexts, and Their Plays* (Newark and London: University of Delaware Press, 1997), pp. 20–50.
2. Park Honan, *Christopher Marlowe: Poet and Spy* (see Further Reading), p. 247.
3. Oscar Wilde, 'The Doer of Good,' in *The Complete Works of Oscar Wilde*, with an Introduction by Vyvyan Holland, 1st Perennial Library edition. Reprint. Originally published London: Collins, 1966, pp. 863–4.
4. Wilde, 'The Doer of Good,' p. 864.

Chapter 6

1. For news stories about Ashley Smith, see www.usatoday.com/news/nation/2005-03-24-smith-reward_x.htm; http://crime.about.com/b/a/156461.htm; and http://en.wikipedia.org/wiki/Ashley_Smith.
2. See www.anncoulter.com/cgi-local/article.cgi?article=49.

Chapter 8

1. Douglas Bruster, '*To Be Or Not To Be*' (London: Continuum, 2007).
2. Harry Frankfurt, *On Bullshit* (Princeton: Princeton University Press, 2005), pp. 47, 54, 61.
3. Ewan Fernie, *Shame in Shakespeare* (London: Routledge, 2001), p. 114.

Chapter 9

1. Robert Ingersoll, in *What's God Got to Do With It?: Robert Ingersoll on Free Thought, Honest Talk, and the Separation of Church and State*, ed. Tim Page (Hanover, NH: Steerforth Press, 2005). p. 16.
2. Frye, *Notebooks*, quoted in Harold Bloom, *Jesus and Yahweh: The Names Divine* (see Further Reading), p. 114.
3. 'The Virgin Mary Underpass Stain,' at www.cnn.com/2005/US/05/06/underpass.virgin.ap/index.html.
4. 'Faith is the secret ...': from *Catholic Encyclopedia*, s.v. 'Heroic Virtue,' at www.newadvent.org/cathen/07292c.htm.

Chapter 11

1. See Jennifer Michael Hecht, *Doubt: A History* (San Francisco: Harper San Francisco, 2003), p. 307.

Chapter 12

1. I owe the observation of this comic moment to Gregory Foran.

Chapter 13

1. The *OED* definition is from Harold Brooks, ed., *A Midsummer Night's Dream* (London: Methuen and Co., 1979).
2. Thanks to Jonathan Lamb for tracking down this quotation.
3. Thanks to Paul Howe for the reference to Bottom here.
4. H. L. Mencken: 'Immortality,' in *H. L. Mencken on Religion*, ed. S. T. Joshi (Amherst, New York: Prometheus Books, 2002), p. 49.

Chapter 14

1. See Daniel C. Matt, trans., *The Essential Kabbalah: The Heart of Jewish Mysticism* (Edison, NJ: Castle Books, 1997), p. 67.
2. Janet Adelman, *The Common Liar: An Essay on Antony and Cleopatra* (New Haven, CT: Yale University Press, 1975).
3. Allen Grossman, 'Holiness,' in *The Long Schoolroom: Lessons in the Bitter Logic of the Poetic Principle* (Ann Arbor, MI: University of Michigan Press, 1997), p. 181.

Further Reading

For my introductory orientation towards unbelief, these works were substantially influential: G. H. Smith, *Atheism: The Case Against God* (Amhurst, NY: Prometheus Books, 1979); the post at DailyKos by 'Darksyde,' called 'Why I am an Atheist,' 15 November 2005 (http://www.dailykos.com/storyonly/2005/11/15/23544/992); and particularly Sam Harris, *The End of Faith: Religion, Terror, and the Future of Reason* (New York: W. W. Norton, 2004). A bracing shot of sensibleness and insight from the perspective of biology comes from Daniel C. Dennett, *Breaking the Spell: Religion as a Natural Phenomenon* (New York: Viking Press, 2006); and, less directly, but importantly, Richard Dawkins, *The Selfish Gene* (Oxford: Oxford University Press, reprint edn, 1999).

The following books have forced me to rethink (in quite different ways) some hidebound notions of Judaism and Christianity: Bertrand Russell, *Why I Am Not a Christian* (New York: Simon and Schuster, 1957); Robert Ingersoll, *Some Mistakes of Moses* (Amherst, NY: Prometheus Books, 1986); Jack Miles, *Christ: A Crisis in the Life of God* (London: William Heinemann, 2001); Harold Bloom, *Jesus and Yahweh: The Names Divine* (New York: Riverhead Books (Penguin), 2005); and Elaine Pagels, *Beyond Belief: The Secret Gospel of Thomas* (New York: Vintage Books, 2003).

Finally, for the subject of religion in Shakespeare and the Renaissance, I have profited from these: Don Cameron Allen, *Doubt's Boundless Sea: Skepticism and Faith in the Renaissance* (Baltimore: Johns Hopkins University Press, 1964); the recent biographies of Christopher Marlowe, by David Riggs: *The World of Christopher Marlowe* (New York: Henry Holt and Co., 2004) and Park Honan, *Christopher Marlowe: Poet and Spy* (Oxford: Oxford University Press, 2005); and Richard H. Popkin, *The History of Skepticism from Erasmus to Spinoza* (Berkeley: University of California Press, 1979). George T. Buckley's classic *Atheism in the English*

Renaissance (Chicago: University of Chicago Press, 1932) provides extremely helpful background to the topic, as does Robert N. Watson's *The Rest is Silence: Death as Annihilation in the English Renaissance* (Berkeley: University of California Press, 1994).

Index

Subjects and Names

Shakespeare Characters